Clifford R. O'Donnell
Joseph R. Ferrari
Editors

Education in Community Psychology: Models for Graduate and Undergraduate Programs

Pre-publication REVIEWS, COMMENTARIES, EVALUATIONS . . .

"This text is unique in its emphasis on undergraduate programs, graduate training, and employment opportunities. It is comprehensive in its coverage. The book is useful for students seeking a major, for graduate students entering the field, and for instructors and advisors who interact with students making career decisions. Moreover, the descriptions of courses and programs may well provide new ideas for instructors seeking to improve their courses."

Murray Levine, JD, PhD
Distinguished Service Professor
Department of Psychology
SUNY Buffalo

More pre-publication
REVIEWS, COMMENTARIES, EVALUATIONS . . .

"This book provides a thoughtful consideration of the many issues involved in community psychology education. The authors ably identify and synthesize the literature on the topic of education and training in community psychology. The book includes a welcome survey of the many different types of training programs in community psychology. The authors honestly explore the difficulties and dilemmas involved in community training as well as the accomplishments. This book should go a long way towards helping to advance the field of community psychology as it enters an exciting new phase of development."

Cary Cherniss, PhD
Professor of Applied Psychology
Rutgers University
Piscataway, NJ

"*Education in Community Psychology: Models for Graduate and Undergraduate Programs* will be an invaluable resource for students seeking graduate training in community psychology. The comparisons of different types of programs, and examination of variations among programs of particular types, will allow students to select training opportunities that best meet their needs. The thoughtful reports on multiple approaches to meeting pedagogical goals and innovations in curricula will also serve faculty who want to improve undergraduate teaching and graduate programs."

Marybeth Shinn, PhD
Professor of Psychology
and Coordinator
Community Doctoral Program
New York University

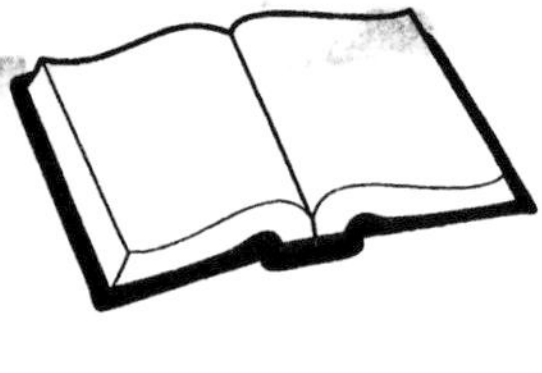

More pre-publication
REVIEWS, COMMENTARIES, EVALUATIONS . . .

"This book is a valuable reference guide for the academic planning a training program in community psychology. It recognizes the community level of analysis that community psychologists use in their work and provides models for training at the undergraduate, masters, and doctoral levels.

. . . This is one of those books in the field that should be on everyone's shelf filled with highlighting and marginal notes."

J. R. Newbrough, PhD
Professor of Psychology
Peabody College
of Vanderbilt University
Nashville, TN

"Chapters in this volume describe programs in all the varieties of community psychology graduate training, at the master's and doctoral level, in community, community-clinical, and interdisciplinary areas. . .

The innovative use of student profiles and perspectives in each chapter provides a feel for the "reality" of each program that cannot be communicated through program descriptions, especially for the values orientation of each program and its place in its own local/regional community . . . Since its founding, community psychology has sought to educate the 'participant-conceptualizer' committed to both community research and social justice. This volume provides a sound road map for that education."

James H. Dalton, Jr., PhD
Professor of Psychology
Bloomsburg University
Bloomsburg, PA

The Haworth Press, Inc.

Education in Community Psychology: Models for Graduate and Undergraduate Programs

The *Prevention & Intervention in the Community* series: *
(formerly the *Prevention in Human Services* series)

- *Families as Nurturing Systems: Support Across the Life Span,* edited by Donald G. Unger and Douglas R. Powell
- *Religion and Prevention in Mental Health: Research, Vision, and Action*, edited by Kenneth I. Pargament, Kenneth I. Maton, and Robert E. Hess
- *Prevention and School Transitions*, edited by Leonard A. Jason, Karen E. Danner, and Karen S. Kurasaki
- *Self-Help and Mutual Aid Groups: International and Multicultural Perspectives,* edited by Francine Lavoie, Thomasina Borkman, and Benjamin Gidron
- *International Approaches to Prevention in Mental Health and Human Services,* edited by Robert E. Hess and Wolfgang Stark
- *Sexual Assault and Abuse: Sociocultural Context of Prevention,* edited by Carolyn F. Swift
- *Preventing Illness Among People with Coronary Heart Disease*, edited by John D. Piette, Robert M. Kaplan, and Joseph R. Ferrari*
- *Adolescent Health Care: Program Designs and Services*, edited by John S. Wodarski, Marvin D. Feit, and Joseph R. Ferrari*
- *Education in Community Psychology: Models for Graduate and Undergraduate Programs*, edited by Clifford R. O'Donnell and Joseph R. Ferrari*

These books were published simultaneously as special thematic issues of *Prevention & Intervention in the Community* and are available bound separately. For further information, call 1-800-HAWORTH (outside US/Canada: 607-722-5857), Fax 1-800-895-0582 (outside US/Canada: 607-771-0012) or e-mail getinfo@haworth.com

Education in Community Psychology: Models for Graduate and Undergraduate Programs

Clifford R. O'Donnell
Joseph R. Ferrari
Editors

The Haworth Press, Inc.
New York • London

Education in Community Psychology: Models for Graduate and Undergraduate Programs has also been published as *Journal of Prevention & Intervention in the Community*, Volume 15, Number 1 1997.

The Haworth Press, Inc., 10 Alice Street, Binghamton, NY 13904-1580 USA

Cover design by Thomas J. Mayshock, Jr.

Library of Congress Cataloging-in-Publication Data

Education in community psychology : models for graduate and undergraduate programs / Clifford R. O'Donnell, Joseph R. Ferrari.

p. cm.

Includes bibliographical references and index.

ISBN 0-7890-0315-5 (alk. paper)

1. Community psychology–Study and teaching. I. O'Donnell, Clifford R. II. Ferrari, Joseph R.

RA790.55.E38 1997 97-759

362.2–dc21 CIP

INDEXING & ABSTRACTING

Contributions to this publication are selectively indexed or abstracted in print, electronic, online, or CD-ROM version(s) of the reference tools and information services listed below. This list is current as of the copyright date of this publication. See the end of this section for additional notes.

- ***Abstracts of Research in Pastoral Care & Counseling***, Loyola College, 7135 Minstrel Way, Suite 101, Columbia, MD 21045
- ***Behavioral Medicine Abstracts,*** University of Washington, School of Social Work, Seattle, WA 98195
- ***Child Development Abstracts & Bibliography***, University of Kansas, 2 Bailey Hall, Lawrence, KS 66045
- ***CNPIEC Reference Guide: Chinese Directory of Foreign Periodicals***, P.O. Box 88, Beijing, Peoples Republic of China
- ***Excerpta Medica/Secondary Publishing Division***, Elsevier Science Inc., Secondary Publishing Division, 655 Avenue of the Americas, New York, NY 10010
- ***Family Studies Database (online and CD/ROM),*** National Information Services Corporation, 306 East Baltimore Pike, 2nd Floor, Media, PA 19063
- ***IBZ International Bibliography of Periodical Literature,*** Zeller Verlag GmbH & Co., P.O.B. 1949, d-49009 Osnabruck, Germany
- ***INTERNET ACCESS (& additional networks) Bulletin Board for Libraries ("BUBL"), coverage of information resources on INTERNET, JANET, and other networks.***
  - JANET X.29:UK.AC.BATH.BUBL or 00006012101300
  - TELNET: BUBL.BATH.AC.UK or 138.38.32.45 login 'bubl'
  - Gopher: BUBL.BATH.AC.UK (138.32.32.45). Port 7070
  - World Wide Web: http: // www.bubl.bath.ac.uk./BUBL/ home.html
  - NISSWAIS: telnetniss.ac.uk (for the NISS gateway)

  The Andersonian Library, Curran Building, 101 St. James Road, Glasgow G4 ONS, Scotland
- ***Mental Health Abstracts (online through DIALOG)***, IFI/Plenum Data Company, 3202 Kirkwood Highway, Wilmington, DE 19808
- ***National Clearinghouse on Child Abuse & Neglect,*** 10530 Rosehaven Street, Suite 400, Fairfax, VA 22030-2804
- ***NIAAA Alcohol and Alcohol Problems Science Database (ETOH),*** National Institute on Alcohol Abuse and Alcoholism, 1400 Eye Street NW, Suite 600, Washington, DC 20005
- ***OT BibSys,*** American Occupational Therapy Foundation, P.O. Box 31220, Bethesda, MD 20824-1220

(continued)

- ***Referativnyi Zhurnal (Abstracts Journal of the Institute of Scientific Information of the Republic of Russia)***, The Institute of Scientific Information, Baltijskaja ul., 14, Moscow A-219, Republic of Russia
- ***RMDB DATABASE (Reliance Medical Information)***, Reliance Medical Information, Inc. (RMI), 100 Putnam Green, Greenwich, CT 06830
- ***Social Planning/Policy & Development Abstracts (SOPODA)***, Sociological Abstracts, Inc., P. O. Box 22206, San Diego, CA 92192-0206
- ***Social Work Abstracts***, National Association of Social Workers, 750 First Street NW, 8th Floor, Washington, DC 20002
- ***Sociological Abstracts (SA)***, Sociological Abstracts, Inc., P. O. Box 22206, San Diego, CA 92192-0206
- ***SOMED (social medicine) Database***, Landes Institut fur Den Offentlichen Gesundheitsdienst NRW, Postfach 20 10 12, D-33548 Bielefeld, Germany
- ***Violence and Abuse Abstracts: A Review of Current Literature on Interpersonal Violence (VAA)***, Sage Publications, Inc., 2455 Teller Road, Newbury Park, CA 91320

SPECIAL BIBLIOGRAPHIC NOTES

related to special journal issues (separates) and indexing/abstracting

- ❑ indexing/abstracting services in this list will also cover material in any "separate" that is co-published simultaneously with Haworth's special thematic journal issue or DocuSerial. Indexing/abstracting usually covers material at the article/chapter level.
- ❑ monographic co-editions are intended for either non-subscribers or libraries which intend to purchase a second copy for their circulating collections.
- ❑ monographic co-editions are reported to all jobbers/wholesalers/approval plans. The source journal is listed as the "series" to assist the prevention of duplicate purchasing in the same manner utilized for books-in-series.
- ❑ to facilitate user/access services all indexing/abstracting services are encouraged to utilize the co-indexing entry note indicated at the bottom of the first page of each article/chapter/contribution.
- ❑ this is intended to assist a library user of any reference tool (whether print, electronic, online, or CD-ROM) to locate the monographic version if the library has purchased this version but not a subscription to the source journal.
- ❑ individual articles/chapters in any Haworth publication are also available through the Haworth Document Delivery Services (HDDS).

Education in Community Psychology: Models for Graduate and Undergraduate Programs

CONTENTS

ALL HAWORTH BOOKS AND JOURNALS ARE PRINTED ON CERTIFIED ACID-FREE PAPER

ABOUT THE EDITORS

Clifford R. O'Donnell, PhD, is Professor of Psychology and Director of the Community Studies Graduate Program at the University of Hawaii. Formerly Chair of the National Council of Program Directors in Community Research and Action, he was the Director of the Center for Youth Research at the University of Hawaii from 1987 until 1993. An Executive Board member of the National Consortium for Children, Families, and the Law, he has published over 100 journal articles, chapters, and technical reports on topics such as delinquency prevention, social networks, programs for at-risk youths, and culturally-compatible forms of community development. He has served as a consultant to the United States Peace Corps in Micronesia and the Zuni Native American Tribe in New Mexico, and has provided program evaluation services to elementary, intermediate, and high schools, correctional facilities, the Family Court, settlement house programs, drug-treatment programs, and Head Start in Hawaii. Dr. O'Donnell has presented invited Congressional testimony and briefings on the U.N. Convention on the Rights of Children, minority over-representation in the justice system, and methods to reduce firearm injuries and deaths. In 1996, he was awarded fellow status in the Society for Commuity Research and Action in "Recognition of his Outstanding Contributions to the Field of Community Research and Action."

Joseph R. Ferrari, PhD, is Visiting Assistant Professor in the Department of Psychology at DePaul University in Chicago, Illinois. The Editor-in-Chief of *Journal of Prevention & Intervention in the Community*, he is the author of three books and nearly 60 research articles. Dr. Ferrari received his PhD from Adelphi University, with a concentration in experimental social-personality psychology. In addition to his interest in mainstream social psychological issues, such as persuasion, attribution theory, and altruism, he has developed several lines of research in social-community psychology.

Graduate Programs and Undergraduate Courses in Community Research and Action

Clifford R. O'Donnell
University of Hawaii

Joseph R. Ferrari
DePaul University

Graduate programs in community research and action reflect the diversity of the field. There are free-standing graduate programs, clinical-community programs, and interdisciplinary programs both within and outside of psychology. Some are master's-level programs, but most are doctoral-level. These categories of programs are by no means exclusive. Some combine free-standing and clinical options, others have interdisciplinary options (O'Donnell, 1994). There are concerns common to all programs and concerns unique to the type of program or to the development of undergraduate courses. The purpose of this volume is to review the various types of graduate programs, along with undergraduate courses in community psychology, with examples of specific programs and courses, to facilitate the development of future graduate programs and undergraduate courses.

The development of additional undergraduate courses in community psychology is one of the most important topics in the field. Since most undergraduates do not continue on to graduate school, any knowledge of

---

[Haworth co-indexing entry note]: "Graduate Programs and Undergraduate Courses in Community Research and Action." O'Donnell, Clifford R., and Joseph R. Ferrari. Co-published simultaneously in *Journal of Prevention & Intervention in the Community* (The Haworth Press, Inc.) Vol. 15, No. 1, 1997, pp. 1-3; and: *Education in Community Psychology: Models for Graduate and Undergraduate Programs* (ed: Clifford R. O'Donnell, and Joseph R. Ferrari.) The Haworth Press, Inc., 1997, pp. 1-3. Single or multiple copies of this article are available for a fee from The Haworth Document Delivery Service [1-800-342-9678, 9:00 a.m. - 5:00 p.m. (EST). E-mail address: getinfo@haworth.com].

community research and action must come from their undergraduate courses. Given the paucity of undergraduate courses in community psychology, most college graduates, even most psychology majors, have little knowledge of the field. Moreover, those who do apply to graduate school are not likely to apply to community graduate programs if they have not been exposed to the field as an undergraduate.

In the development of an undergraduate course, it is necessary, of course, to consider the course content. Given the diversity of the field and its interdisciplinary nature, this is a more formidable task than is true of most courses. It involves the definition of the field, its values, ethics, topics, theories, and methods, all of which differ, often sharply, from other fields of psychology. Then there is the question of whether an appreciation of community psychology can be developed without any field experience and how to integrate such experience with other coursework (Ferrari & Geller, 1994). All of these issues are addressed by O'Sullivan.

The issue of the role for a community psychologist is particularly pressing for masters-level graduate programs. For students who do not continue on to doctoral programs, there are questions of their role and the marketability of their degree. For those who do enter doctoral programs, there are issues in the articulation of their coursework, theses, and practica. These topics are addressed by Goldstein and Woltz.

Graduate programs in clinical-community psychology continue to dominate the field by their number (comprising about half of all community graduate programs), their attraction to students interested in becoming licensed psychologists, their accreditation by the American Psychological Association, and the perceived employability of their graduates. Professional psychology, however, is undergoing many changes. The new guidelines and procedures for accreditation now permit other types of professional programs to apply for accreditation and the increase in graduates from clinical programs, especially from professional schools, has reduced the chances of clinical students obtaining accredited internships and, some predict, diminished future employment possibilities. In addition, managed-care is reducing the lucrativeness of private practice and the drive for prescriptive privileges may increase the medicalization of clinical psychology. All of these factors contribute toward a greater emphasis on mental health issues in clinical-community programs. The changes taking place are fascinating and have important implications for professional psychology. They are addressed by Meissen and Slavich.

The term free-standing community program refers to doctoral programs that are located within psychology departments without being attached to another specialty area of psychology, such as clinical or social. Free of the need to include courses and practica from another specialty, free-standing programs have developed curricula with the greatest focus on community psychology. These programs typically are designed for students who do not wish to become licensed psychologists or engage primarily in individual treatment. Instead, they are designed to attract students who are interested in program/community development, analysis, prevention/intervention, evaluation, and related research. Gensheimer and Diebold provide a thorough examination of free-standing programs.

Interdisciplinary programs have the fewest ties to mental health issues. Since most other disciplines do not focus on mental health, most of those that join to form community research and action programs allow a greater emphasis on other domains of human activity. Indeed, some interdisciplinary programs do not include psychology, much less clinical psychology, programs. When the Division of Community Psychology became the Society for Community Research and Action, its members sought to include community-oriented members from disciplines other than psychology. So too, the Council of Program Directors in Community Research and Action (formerly the Council of Community Psychology Program Directors) has begun to recruit community-oriented programs in disciplines in addition to psychology.

For these reasons, it is the interdisciplinary programs that hold the most promise for innovation in graduate education and the greatest potential for developing community research and action into an interdisciplinary field. For an examination of the characteristics and future prospects of this developing field, as represented by graduate programs, we are fortunate to include the article by Reynolds.

Most community graduate programs are in North America. To present a different perspective, Thomas, Neill, and Robertson review the history and content of their program at the University of Waikato, New Zealand and its ties to community organizations. In New Zealand there is less concern about non-clinical professional roles and employment because graduates of the community program can register as psychologists. This experience may provide a model for the future development of professional psychology.

In each of these articles, the authors present a sample of student perspectives and some thoughts on the creation of community undergraduate courses and graduate programs. Following these articles, the major issues are reviewed.

REFERENCES

Ferrari, J. R., & Geller, E. S. (1994). Developing future caregivers by integrating research and community service. *The Community Psychologist, 27,* 12-13.

O'Donnell, C. R. (1994). Community studies: A multi-disciplinary program. *The Community Psychologist, 27,* 8-10.

Undergraduate Courses in Community Psychology: Issues, Paradigms, and Experiences

Michael J. O'Sullivan

Loyola Marymount University

SUMMARY. The value of the undergraduate course in community psychology for students, faculty, and the field itself is discussed. Following an overview of pedagogical issues and strategies in teaching this course, examples of successful course outlines as well as student reactions are presented. Recommendations are made for faculty planning to teach community psychology on the undergraduate level. *[Article copies available for a fee from The Haworth Document Delivery Service: 1-800-342-9678. E-mail address: getinfo@haworth.com]*

As a subdiscipline within the science of psychology, community psychology represents a paradigm shift away from the usual levels of analysis, research methods, assumptions about the causes of problems, and

---

Address correspondence to Michael J. O'Sullivan, Department of Psychology, Loyola Marymount University, 7900 Loyola Boulevard, Los Angeles, CA 90045-8405.

The author thanks Cheryl Grills, Loyola Marymount University, and Nancy Worsham, Gonzaga University, for sharing their experiences in teaching undergraduate Community Psychology; Kristi Gonsalves and Steve Wachs for their contributions to this article; and Clifford O'Donnell, University of Hawaii, for his invaluable editorial advice.

[Haworth co-indexing entry note]: "Undergraduate Courses in Community Psychology: Issues, Paradigms, and Experiences." O'Sullivan, Michael J. Co-published simultaneously in *Journal of Prevention & Intervention in the Community* (The Haworth Press, Inc.) Vol. 15, No. 1, 1997, pp. 5-16; and: *Education in Community Psychology: Models for Graduate and Undergraduate Programs* (ed: Clifford R. O'Donnell, and Joseph R. Ferrari) The Haworth Press, Inc., 1997, pp. 5-16. Single or multiple copies of this article are available for a fee from The Haworth Document Delivery Service [1-800-342-9678, 9:00 a.m. - 5:00 p.m. (EST). E-mail address: getinfo@haworth.com].

approaches to practice and intervention. If these profound shifts appear somewhat uncharacteristic of psychology itself, how much more so do they seem innovative and radically different for the undergraduate psychology major?

The standard undergraduate psychology curriculum teaches students the biopsychosocial model of human behavior. However the regular courses in experimental methods, neuroscience, cognitive, developmental, learning, personality, and abnormal seem to focus much more on the psychological and biological. Although a course in social psychology helps the student to think in terms of groups and interpersonal behavior, the social dimension of the biopsychosocial model tends to fade in the minds of most psychology majors. They learn to think about human behavior in terms of the individual somewhat in isolation from the social systems in which that person lives and functions.

The course in community psychology teaches students that many of the problems people experience stem from long-term interactions with social settings and systems, that prevention can be a more effective intervention than treatment, and that social support networks and non-professionals can reach and benefit far more people than mental health professionals seeing clients in offices. The course introduces students to micro- and macro-levels of analysis, quasi-experimental designs, action research, and community needs assessment.

Not only are such paradigm shifts "eye-opening" and stimulating for the students, community psychology instructors find these concepts exciting to teach. In the majority of schools offering undergraduate community psychology, the course is presented as an upper-division elective, i.e., an optional course for students in their final years in college. This reality provides the professor with an opportunity to employ an innovative pedagogy in the course's content and structure.

ISSUES IN COURSE DESIGN AND PEDAGOGY

A good sampling of the variety of materials and syllabi for undergraduate courses in community psychology from across the country is available from the Community Psychology Education Connection Clearinghouse.[1] From both the information available from the Clearinghouse and conversations with several faculty teaching undergraduate community courses, it seems that there are three paramount issues that instructors face when designing such courses. One must decide (a) how to integrate presenting the values of community psychology together with the theories, methods, and applications of this field; (b) whether or not to require a field placement or practicum experience in the course; and (c) the size of the course section.

Topics and Values

The topics usually covered in undergraduate community psychology courses include some combination of the following: definition and history of community psychology, values and theories underpinning the field, research and assessment methods used, ecological and environmental approaches, prevention and health promotion, mental health and health care delivery systems, empowerment and self-help, social support and community participation, social problems and social change, multicultural and gender issues, and homelessness and immigration.

To cover these topics, several community psychology textbooks are available (Duffy & Wong, 1996; Heller, Price, Reinharz, Riger, & Wandersman, 1984; Levine & Perkins, 1997; Orford, 1992). Overall, both students and faculty have found the available textbooks quite limited in their ability to capture the students' interest. However the newest text (Duffy & Wong, 1996) may have more success in this regard. Of course one can also put together a collection of articles and/or book chapters to accomplish the same goal. In fact, most faculty seem to use a combination of textbook(s) and readings to cover the topics they include in their courses. Dalton and O'Donnell (1996) have assembled a most useful reading list in community psychology which includes both books and articles organized by both standard and special topics in the discipline (e.g., theory, methods, empowerment, social support).

The values underlying these core topics both resonate with the humanitarian disposition of many psychology students and can challenge them to reevaluate their career plans. From its origins in the Kennedy-Johnson War on Poverty, community psychology has combined social science and social justice. Students learn that environments can not only cause problems but also be changed, that individual problems are not always a maladjustment to a benign social situation, and that populations such as the poor and chronically mentally ill face complex and multidimensional problems that encompass a variety of social institutions and public policies. Undergraduates readily recognize empowerment, promoting a psychological sense of community, and respecting cultural diversity as value-laden constructs.

The instructor faces the challenge of how to present these values in the context of the theory and practice of community psychology. The pedagogy employed can present the theory and methods as either (a) relatively value-free, or (b) infused with values that challenge and motivate the students' own sense of social justice and desire for change. In other words, either students leave the course with simply an academic understanding of community psychology, or students come alive in the course and seek to apply their learning to "real world" situations.

Faculty report that how they choose to integrate the values and academic content of their courses greatly influences the learning experience for their students. Their students finish the course either only "knowing about" community psychology, or "thinking and acting like" community psychologists.

Field Placements

Those faculty requiring field placements or practica in their courses have found that community psychology is best taught by doing (Jason, 1984; McLean, Johnson, & Eblen, 1977; O'Sullivan, 1993; Rossi, 1975). Both the values and content of community psychology take on life for students when they acquire hands-on experiences working with people who in fact are experiencing negative impacts from actual social institutions or systems.

What seems especially rewarding both for students and faculty is the opportunity for students to apply what they have learned in ways that benefit constructive change in the lives of the people they serve. This "service-learning" leaves a positive impression in the experience of students that endures beyond the end of the semester or quarter (Glenwick & Chabot, 1991; McCluskey-Fawcett & Green, 1992; O'Sullivan, 1993).

Faculty report that the majority of students who have had a field placement evaluate it as the "best" or "most important" aspect of the community psychology course. However, some students–albeit few–evaluate the experience negatively. The field experience itself tends to be polarizing. Students committed to community psychology values find the fieldwork rewarding; otherwise it becomes personally threatening and difficult (McLean et al., 1977; O'Sullivan, 1993).

The polarizing nature of the field placement as well as the practical difficulties of implementing such a requirement present the instructor with a difficult choice when designing the undergraduate course. Arranging such placements for the first time requires considerable time and energy. Some academic institutions have established community service programs that provide invaluable assistance, whereas other schools do not (O'Sullivan, 1993). Nevertheless, the available literature not only offers the instructor many practical suggestions on how to proceed with field placements, but also confirms that the benefits derived justify the efforts expended (Glenwick & Chabot, 1991; Jason, 1984; McCluskey-Fawcett & Green, 1992; McLean et al., 1977; O'Sullivan, 1993; VandeCreek & Fleischer, 1984).

Class Size

If the course pedagogy includes class participation, discussions, and field placements, then experienced faculty recommend that course sections involve no more than 15 students. Greater numbers of students limit class interaction as well as unduly complicate the process of securing sufficient numbers of valuable and viable field placements. On the other hand, the class size can be much larger if the pedagogy primarily consists of lectures, papers, and student class presentations/projects.

To summarize the key aspects in structuring the undergraduate course in community psychology, the professor needs to consider the three issues of values/topics, field placement, and class size. These concerns interact with one another to profoundly influence both the teaching and the learning processes. Decisions in one of these areas most likely will facilitate decisions in the others, which in turn will determine the outcome of the course.

SAMPLE COURSE OUTLINES

Several examples of how different faculty have designed their undergraduate community psychology courses may provide models for how the issues discussed above can be managed successfully. The three specific courses presented below received positive evaluations from both faculty and students.

Sample A

In an earlier article (O'Sullivan, 1993) I provided a more complete description of my own undergraduate course in community psychology. The course was designed to give students an integrative learning experience that combined academic coursework (textbook, variety of journal articles, lectures), exposure to current sociopolitical affairs (reading of the metropolitan daily newspaper), and personal experience working with individuals living on the fringes of society (practicum involving placements with one of three populations: the homeless, chronically mentally ill, and refugees and/or illegal immigrants).

The textbook (Heller et al., 1984) and other readings covered such topics as the methods and values of community psychology; the effects of social and environmental factors on behavior as it occurs at individual, group, organizational, and societal levels; stress and social support; prevention and health promotion; consultation, citizen participation, empowerment, and social change; and ethical issues in community interventions. Other readings (research articles, government reports, the daily newspaper) provided valuable and current information concerning the populations that students were encountering in their field placements. This course worked much better with a smaller class size (15 or fewer students).

Since that article was written and following a sabbatical, several modifications were introduced into the course. Due to the many required hours involved in field placements, students now earned four rather than three semester hour credits for the course. However, the principal change involved orienting the course much more toward inculcating in students the values of community psychology. This was accomplished primarily by changing and refocusing the required texts for the course. The community psychology textbook was replaced with two books on social analysis and societal values (Bellah, Madsen, Sullivan, Swidler, & Tipton, 1991; Jencks, 1992). The course objectives, structure, and target populations (for the field placement sites) remained the same. The standard topics presented in community psychology textbooks were covered in a variety of journal articles and lectures.

Sample B

A professor whose own professional activity and academic research interests have long been in community oriented substance abuse prevention programs sought to teach an undergraduate course in community psychology for two principal reasons: (a) to expose students to a different perspective in psychology–in which both theory and research expanded beyond "the individual"; and (b) to help students make psychology come alive by applying it to real world situations (C. Grills, personal communication, February 14, 1996). The course was limited to 15 students and included both academic/didactic and field placement components.

The academic element included lectures, discussions, a textbook (Orford, 1992), and a variety of other scholarly readings. Over the course of the semester various weeks were devoted to defining community psychology, the challenge of multicultural diversity, ecological and environmental influences, defining community problems, promoting community empowerment, social support and social control, and applied research and evaluation.

The field placement component of this course was innovative in combining two levels of this experience. First, students had their own individual field placements. Second, the class as a whole worked step-by-step through a "real world" intervention in an ethnically diverse and poverty-stricken neighborhood in a large metropolitan city. In this class project, university faculty and students helped empower neighborhood residents as they sought to define and obtain public safety in their community.

Both the professor and the students found this course both educationally and personally fulfilling. Whereas at the beginning of the semester students seemed unable to reframe issues from individual-alone to individual-system interaction, by the conclusion of the course they became adept at doing so. The professor was gratified both by this transition in the students' thinking and by the students' excitement in applying their learning in the service of others. However, the textbook surfaced as a problem needing attention. The students struggled with the text and it failed to capture their attention and interest (C. Grills, personal communication, February 14, 1996).

Sample C

Prevention and community mental health form the clinical background of another professor reporting a gratifying and challenging experience teaching undergraduate community psychology (N. Worsham, personal communication, February 28, 1996). The course presented students with substantial amounts of theory and research, and then required students to work in teams designing viable prevention and/or community intervention programs addressing a specific problem. Students were required to (a) base their programs on reviews of the literature, and (b) design an evaluation to assess the impact of their program. Teams made class presentations on their programs as well as wrote papers summarizing their programs and research base.

The course required two textbooks, and seemed to be structured around their content. The first half of the semester was devoted to an overview of community psychology and included material from Orford (1992), special readings, and several guests addressing community and public policy topics. The second part of the semester focused on prevention programs addressing specific community problems (e.g., substance abuse, teenage pregnancy, road safety). This latter half of the course consisted of readings from Glenwick and Jason (1993), and student team presentations.

Although both faculty and students evaluated the course quite positively, the professor continues to restructure the course due to the class size, field placement, and textbook issues discussed above. Initially presented in a lecture format with more than 40 students, the course thereafter was offered as a seminar limited to 15 students. The smaller class size again was identified as providing a more profound educational experience.

The research based prevention programs students designed constituted an enriching but limited learning experience. However both the students and professor realized that the opportunity to implement their programs in the service of actual community needs would have provided a more complete educational experience. Of course, the problem remains how to accomplish all this in one course. Consequently the professor now suggests a two course sequence. The first course would include the theory and research. The second semester would consist of a practicum involving the application of their knowledge at a paraprofessional level (N. Worsham, personal communication, February 28, 1996).

STUDENT REACTIONS

In preparing this article two former students in two different community psychology courses were interviewed. One individual (male) had just completed the course (viz., Sample B above), whereas the other person (female) had taken the course (viz., Sample A above) nearly four years earlier during her final year of college.

Male. This student is a psychology major and took the course in the fall semester of his final year in college. He knew that his interests and strengths were in working with and serving people. In several other psychology courses he briefly encountered community perspectives, but did not have a firm idea of this field. The course attracted him because of his own interests in neighborhoods and how such communities have their own "personalities." Although aware of the required practicum working with underserved populations, as he enrolled in the course he had little idea of community psychology's action and prevention orientations, applied research, cultural diversity, and empowerment concerns.

The community psychology course evolved into an exciting and profound experience for this college senior. At first he struggled with the paradigm shift, but eventually found himself thinking in terms of person-system interactions. His field placement entailed working in a program for homeless families. This experience as well as the class project working with the inner-city neighborhood became the "highlights" of the course for him. He found that these "real life" experiences, the academic readings, and the class discussions all informed each other.

For him, psychology took on a solution-oriented approach to urban/community problems. When asked to compare this course to others in his psychology major, he stated that community psychology did not seem as scientific and research oriented as other subdisciplines in the field (e.g., experimental, cognitive, abnormal). As a result, he would not recommend the course to other students whose primary interests focused on scientific research. However, he would recommend the course to those seeking practical applications of psychology in attacking the causes of many problems faced by urban communities.

Having completed the course, this student found himself rethinking his future career. Whereas he had planned to apply for graduate study in counseling or clinical psychology, he now was considering pursuing graduate degrees in either social welfare or community psychology.

Female. During her undergraduate career, this individual majored in English literature and minored in psychology. During her senior year she was attracted to the community psychology course by its favorable reputation among other students, the combination of theory and practice, and an opportunity in the field placement to integrate her academics with serving people on the margins of society.

As she looked back over the years since graduating from college, she reported that the most "crucial" aspects of the course were the practicum and the required reading of the daily newspaper. The practicum taught her that she could actually use her education to serve people who seemed powerless. On campus she read, studied, and learned in the academic setting. Off campus she applied her learning and saw it take on life as she worked with people who had no political voice. The newspaper exposed her to issues affecting the community, and taught her that she could remain informed as long as she made this reading a regular practice.

Her experience in the course did not so much change her career and/or worldview, but rather helped solidify them. She found that the values she encountered in community psychology resonated with her own religious faith and practices. Community psychology not only helped her see "the big picture" but also provided her with social change strategies to complement her religious tradition's concept of the "common good."

She recommended the course to most of her fellow students, whether or not they were psychology majors. Following graduation she spent two years in a national volunteer program living and working with underserved populations. Currently she works with college students in a community service program helping undergraduates learn how to apply their academic training in ways that serve populations in need.

CONCLUDING COMMENTS

It seems that most faculty who teach this course not only have endorsed the paradigm shift that community psychology presents, but also have acquired academic and professional experiences in this area. As might be expected, faculty convey to their students both their knowledge of and enthusiasm for community psychology.

As one considers teaching an undergraduate course in community psychology, one might best follow the methods of the discipline itself and first conduct a needs assessment. Is there a perceived need both by faculty and students for such a course in the curriculum? Given the nature of most academic institutions, departmental approval for a new course will be contingent upon faculty support. The longevity of the course will depend on sufficient student enrollment.

With the decision made to proceed with developing the community psychology course, perhaps the next step involves contacting the Education Connection Clearinghouse for sample undergraduate course syllabi. Class size, field placement, and textbook issues deserve careful attention. If the instructor intends to teach both the values and methods of community psychology, then both a small class size and a field placement are recommended. To convey the "heart and mind" of community psychology, class discussions and hands-on experience must complement academic reading and writing.

If one decides to require a practicum experience, inquire whether one's institution has an established community service program for students. If so, establish a relationship with that program to facilitate the practicum. If such a program does not exist, then review the literature for suggestions on developing field placements (Fernald et al., 1982; Jason, 1984; McCluskey-Fawcett & Green, 1992; O'Sullivan, 1993; VandeCreek & Fleischer, 1984). Many urban and rural communities have resource directories available which will provide professors with an overview of the area's agencies and/or services which might serve as appropriate sites for practicum experiences. Special attention must be given to having proper supervision of students on-site during their practicum.

Regardless of whether the framework is lecture or seminar, one or two semesters, finding appropriate reading remains a concern. Faculty need to be judicious in selecting their required readings. The Dalton and O'Donnell (1996) reading list merits attention. In each of the three sample courses presented above, the faculty reported that the students expressed grave reservations about their respective community psychology textbooks. In each case, the faculty in subsequent semesters replaced the textbooks with other readings. A strong need seems to exist for an undergraduate textbook in this field which can capture the students' interest and imagination.

Unique aspects of either the course objectives (e.g., inculcating community psychology values) or its requirements (e.g., practica) merit special attention when evaluating the course. Faculty will want to know which pedagogical methods were effective in meeting the objectives for the majority of the students, and which methods were not. Similarly, before offering the course again it is important to assess which field placements provided students with valuable experiences and which did not–including both students' evaluations of their supervision and supervisors' appraisals of the students' work.

The undergraduate course in community psychology can be an exciting educational experience for both faculty and students. Although not commonly found in the undergraduate psychology curriculum, this course both enriches students and gives vitality to the field itself.

NOTE

1. Community Psychology Education Connection Clearinghouse, c/o James H. Dalton, Department of Psychology, Bloomsburg University, Bloomsburg, PA 17815 (phone: 717-389-4475).

REFERENCES

Bellah, R. N., Madsen, R., Sullivan, W. M., Swidler, A., & Tipton, S. M. (1991). *The good society.* New York: Knopf.

Dalton, J., & O'Donnell, C. R. (1996). Suggested readings in community psychology. *The Community Psychologist* (Special Supplement).

Duffy, K. G., & Wong, F. Y. (1996). *Community psychology.* Boston: Allyn & Bacon.

Fernald, C. D., Tedeschi, R. G., Siegfried, W. D., Gilmore, D. C., Grimsley, D. L., & Chipley, B. (1982). Designing and managing an undergraduate practicum course in psychology. *Teaching of Psychology, 9,* 155-160.

Glenwick, D. S., & Chabot, D. R. (1991). The undergraduate clinical child psychology course: Bringing students to the real world and the real world to students. *Teaching of Psychology, 18,* 21-24.

Glenwick, D. S., & Jason, L. A. (Eds.). (1993). *Promoting health and mental health in children, youth, and families.* New York: Springer.

Heller, K., Price, R. H., Reinharz, S., Riger, S., & Wandersman, A. (1984). *Psychology and community change: Challenges of the Future* (2nd ed.). Homewood, IL: Dorsey Press.

Jason, L. A. (1984). Developing undergraduates' skills in behavioral interventions. *Journal of Community Psychology, 12,* 130-139.

Jencks, C. (1992). *Rethinking social policy: Race, poverty, and the underclass.* Cambridge, MA: Harvard.

Levine, M., & Perkins, D. V. (1997). *Principles of community psychology: Perspectives and applications.* New York: Oxford University Press.
McCluskey-Fawcett, K., & Green, P. (1992). Using community service to teach developmental psychology. *Teaching of Psychology, 19,* 150-152.
McLean, C., Johnson, J., & Eblen, C. (1977). Teaching community psychology to undergraduate students. *Journal of Community Psychology, 5,* 313-318.
Orford, J. (1992). *Community psychology: Theory and practice.* New York: Wiley.
O'Sullivan, M. J. (1993). Teaching undergraduate community psychology: Integrating the classroom and the surrounding community. *Teaching of Psychology, 20,* 80-83.
Rossi, A. M. (1975). Community psychology at the undergraduate level. *Journal of Community Psychology, 3,* 305-308.
VandeCreek, L., & Fleischer, M. (1984). The role of practicum in the undergraduate psychology curriculum. *Teaching of Psychology, 11,* 9-14.

Master's Degree Programs in Community Psychology: Why, Where and How

Marc B. Goldstein
James J. Woltz

Central Connecticut State University

SUMMARY. This article provides a brief overview of master's programs in community psychology including a discussion of role issues facing master's level community psychologists and a description of the ecological context of 6 such programs. We also provide an in-depth look at two of these programs (Penn State Harrisburg, Sage Graduate School) including comments from current and former students. Finally, we conclude with some observations on how to start up a Master's program in community psychology. *[Article copies available for a fee from The Haworth Document Delivery Service: 1-800-342-9678. E-mail address: getinfo@haworth.com]*

The role of the master's level psychologist has been a controversial one in psychology. The debate on this issue reflects both the general lack of clarity about the purpose of master's degrees (Glazer, 1986) as well as turf issues between master's and doctoral level psychologists. Most of the debate has been focused on issues around delivery of clinical services

---

Address correspondence to Marc B. Goldstein, Department of Psychology, Central Connecticut State University, 1615 Stanley Street, New Britain, CT 06050-4010.

[Haworth co-indexing entry note]: "Master's Degree Programs in Community Psychology: Why, Where and How." Goldstein, Marc B., and James J. Woltz. Co-published simultaneously in *Journal of Prevention & Intervention in the Community* (The Haworth Press, Inc.) Vol. 15, No. 1, 1997, pp. 17-30; and: *Education in Community Psychology: Models for Graduate and Undergraduate Programs* (ed: Clifford R. O'Donnell, and Joseph R. Ferrari.) The Haworth Press, Inc., 1997, pp. 17-30. Single or multiple copies of this article are available for a fee from The Haworth Document Delivery Service [1-800-342-9678, 9:00 a.m. - 5:00 p.m. (EST). E-mail address: getinfo@haworth.com].

(e.g., Trent, 1993), an issue that will likely become more heated with the advent of managed care. Issues about the marketability of master's level community psychologists in comparison with other master's level individuals (e.g., MSWs, MFT, Master's in Counseling) have also been raised (Hoffnung, Morris & Jex, 1986).

The present article provides a brief overview of master's programs in community psychology based on interviews with five program directors[1] as well as our own observations. We begin with a discussion of role issues facing master's level community psychologists, followed by a description of the ecological context of these programs and the challenges they face. We also provide an in-depth look at the graduate programs at Penn State Harrisburg and Sage Graduate School, one of The Sage Colleges. Finally, we conclude with some observations on how to start up a master's program in community psychology.

WHAT ROLE DO MA COMMUNITY PSYCHOLOGISTS FILL?

The marginality of the community psychologist role has been noted by Silverman (1978) and others (e.g., Kelly, 1970). Indeed, as Rappaport (1981) stated in his seminal article on empowerment and the value of championing unpopular perspectives: "when most of the people agree with you, worry!" (p. 3). At the master's level, community psychologists compete head-to-head with individuals completing master's degrees in more well-known specialties, such as counseling or social work, which adds to the anxiety.

Master's level community psychologists do get jobs, but with a wide variety of job titles. Much of the appeal of these programs appears to be among more mature students who have previous experience (and frustration) working in human service systems. Most of the program directors indicated that students generally expressed anxiety about the marketability of their degrees early in their graduate education, but typically became more comfortable as their training progressed.

The six programs examined here each train their students for different roles (see Table 1). Despite the different roles listed in the second column of Table 1, an underlying theme for all the programs was helping students develop a "systems perspective" in the way they approached problems and issues in the community. Indeed, program directors felt that the strength of their degree, when compared with other master's-trained individuals, was that students could conceptualize issues in a multi-dimensional way, a skill valued by many administrators in human service settings and the multiple publics which they serve. Moreover, while all programs included research courses as part of their curricula, the focus was clearly on applied research, e.g., needs assessment, program evaluation, the qualitative/quantitative study of a particular community issue.

The Ecology of MA Programs

Beyond the roles for which they trained students, we also looked at the ecological context of these programs. We examined student characteristics as well as issues of support from their departmental colleagues and the university as a whole.

As indicated in Table 1, three of the programs are composed primarily of full-time students, while three serve predominantly part-time students. Several of the part-time programs actively discouraged full-time students; this reflected both the desire to have students actively working in community settings as well as limited financial resources available to support students. While all programs had monies from assistantships or grants to support a small number of students, most students had to pay their own way.

At the department level, most programs reported strong collegial support, but indicated that this was a developmental process. When first started, the community programs were strongly identified with particular faculty who, in turn, made concerted efforts to integrate other department members into the operation of the program.

One program was not housed in a psychology department, but in a behavioral science division that also included sociology. The program director noted that his colleagues felt comfortable with the action research orientation of the division. On the other hand, the psychology department maintains a separate master's program that is more clinical in focus.

Most programs also reported university support. Although these programs are not "cash cows" for the university (the largest program reported taking about 16 students per year), Deans and Academic Vice-Presidents were supportive of their mission. It should be noted that only Penn State Harrisburg and Wilfrid Laurier University, have doctoral level programs in any discipline.

Most programs had a small number of assistantships to support students, and several programs reported that they had individual faculty who had external grants that supported students. Interestingly, 4 of the 6 universities had research and/or community service institutes affiliated with them, and program directors noted that these provided research/consulting opportunities for faculty and students.

TABLE 1. Master's Degree Programs

Program Characteristics (1996)

Institution	Role Preparation	Number of Core Faculty	Program Hours for Degree	Percent of Full-Time Students
Central Connecticut State University	primary preventionists	3	36	10
Mansfield University	rural community/clinical psychologists	3	43	90
Penn State Harrisburg	social change agents	5	36	28
Sage Graduate School	social problem solvers	4	42-51	15
University of New Haven	generalists in human service	3	42 (trimesters)	70
Wilfrid Laurier University	research consultants & social change agents	4	24	80

A Profile of Two Programs

The next section details the well-regarded master's programs at Penn State Harrisburg and Sage Graduate School (Troy, NY). Penn State Harrisburg (PSH) is an upper division school (juniors, seniors, master's level programs) with approximately 3500 students that is part of the multi-campus Penn State system, while Sage Graduate School (Sage) is a small, (about 2000 students) private liberal arts college offering A.A., B.A. and master's level programs.

The graduate program at PSH, which leads to a Masters of Community Psychology, started in 1975. The current program

> emphasizes planned social change . . . [and] equips students with skills useful in coping with the multifaceted problems facing communities. Students learn (a) to assess problems at the level of communities or organizations, (b) to plan and implement possible solutions to these problems, and (c) to evaluate the effectiveness of solutions. (Master of Community Psychology program flyer)

Program Requirements

In the 36 credit program (see Table 2, left column), all students take 8 required courses, and then select an additional 9 credit hours from either the Human Services Management Concentration or an Individual Concentration (see Tables 3 and 3a). Twenty-four of the 36 credits must be at the 500 level (500 level courses are open only to graduate students; 400 level courses can be taken by seniors and graduate students).

The Practicum and Master's Paper are key requirements of the program. Students take a total of 9 credits in these two courses; in consultation with faculty, they determine the relative emphasis each will have (3 or 6 credits) based on their needs for skill development. Students strong in field experience but with little research background emphasize the Master's Paper (research), while those with strong research backgrounds but little field work would choose the reverse.

The Practicum course requires students to design a project/intervention that is likely to have a measurable impact on some target population. The design and implementation of this project typically takes a full academic year and occurs while students work (sometimes on a volunteer basis) in a variety of human service settings, e.g., administrative office of a county mental health program, neighborhood center.

Master's Papers are often focused around a field experience or a specific community research problem. Some recent papers have examined situa-

TABLE 2. Required Courses: Penn State Harrisburg and Sage Graduate School

Penn State Harrisburg		Sage Graduate School	
CMPSY 500	Theories and Issues in Community Psychology	PSY 551	Introduction to Community Psychology (Required)
CMPSY 510	Change Processes	PSY 558[2]	Community-Based Prevention and Social Change
SCLSC 470	Advanced Statistical & Design Methods	PSY 562[2]	Community Mental Health
CMPSY 511	Social Impacts on Psychological Functioning	PSY 564[2]	Community Process and Social Ecology
CMPSY 520	Techniques in Action Research	PSY 565[2]	Community Consultation Services
CMPSY 521	Roles and Methods in Community Psychology	PSY 563	Behavior Research Methods (Required)
CMPSY 522[1]	Practicum (3-6 credits)	PSY 581	Program Evaluation (Required)
CMPSY 594[1]	Master's Paper (3-6 credits)	PSY 589	Thesis or PSY 590 Research Seminar (1 required)

[1]Student must take a total of 9 credit hours in these 2 courses
[2]Student must take 3 of these courses

TABLE 3. Elective Track Options: Penn State Harrisburg and Sage Graduate School

Penn State Harrisburg	Sage Graduate School	
Human Services Management Concentration	General Track	Chemical Dependency Track
3 courses from: Public Organization & Management Governmental Fiscal Decision Making Personnel Management: Public & Non-Profit Sectors Management Information Systems Organizational Behavior Governmental Financial Management ***or*** Individual Concentration Student works with faculty advisor to select 3 courses from Behavioral Science and/or other faculties to reflect student's particular interests, e.g., criminal justice, urban sociology, women studies	Personality Theory or Developmental Psychology Abnormal Psychology ***plus 4 courses from:*** Personality Theory & Research Group Dynamics Developmental Psychology Counseling Psychological Assessment Sources & Outcomes of Stress in Children and Their Families Perspectives on Aging Externship	Developmental Psychology Abnormal Psychology The Psychopharmacology of Drugs and Alcohol The Illness of Alcoholism/Addiction Counseling the Alcoholic/Addictive Family Counseling the Alcoholic/Addictive Person Group Counseling the Alcoholic/Addictive Internship in an Alcohol/Drug Program Current Professional Issues in Alcohol and Substance Abuse Counseling

TABLE 3a. Elective Track Options: Sage Graduate School

Child Care and Children's Services Track	Community Counseling Track
Developmental Psychology	Counseling
Counseling	Group Counseling
Sources and Outcomes of Stress in Children and Their Families	Family Counseling
Family Counseling: A Systems Perspective	Survey of Counseling Applications in the Community
	Practicum
	Developmental Psychology
	Abnormal Psychology
	Externship
plus 3 courses from:	***plus 1 course from the following*:**
Formation and Administration of Human Services Policy	Psychological Assessment
Principles of Finance and Budgeting	Sources and Outcomes of Stress in Children and their Families
Administrative Organization and Behavior	The Illness of Alcoholism/Addiction
Human Services Delivery System	
Externship	

tionally-induced psychological stress among jurors, changing prejudicial attitudes through intergroup contact, and developing a support group for infertile people.

Faculty

The 5 faculty who teach the required courses come from psychology and sociology, while courses in the Human Services Management concentration are taught principally by those with backgrounds in Public Administration. Students who choose to create an Individual Concentration can be exposed to faculty from a wide range of disciplines.

Students

PSH draws the majority of its students from the greater Harrisburg area. Since many of the students work full-time in government or human service settings, all 500 level courses are offered in the evening. About 95% of the students attend part-time and take 1 or 2 courses per term, while full-time students usually take 3 courses per term.

Because of the intensity of the Practicum and Master's Paper requirements, part-time students typically take 6 to 7 semesters to complete the degree, while full-time students often need 5 or more semesters. Since the program's inception, approximately 150 students have earned degrees.

Admission Requirements

All applicants must: (1) have completed a baccalaureate degree from an accredited institution, (2) have a 3.00 GPA or higher (on a 4 point scale) during their junior and senior years, (3) submit Graduate Record Examination Scores (Verbal, Analytical and quantitative Reasoning), (4) prepare a 500 word letter highlighting significant community or work experience along with career objectives, and (5) provide names, addresses and telephone numbers of 3 references. While most applicants have degrees in psychology, sociology or related disciplines, applicants from other backgrounds are encouraged to apply (particularly if they have had experience working on planned social change activities), but may be asked to take additional courses to strengthen their background.

Other Factors

Several other factors contribute to the vitality of the program. These include being located in the state capital with its high concentration of government offices and policy-makers, and its collaboration with the Center for Community Action and Research, a campus-based, applied research arm of the university.

STUDENT'S PERSPECTIVE

We interviewed a current student and a recent graduate to get their perspectives on the PSH program. Ms. H, a part-time student in her second year, came to the program after working in a hospital setting for several years. She was attracted to PSH by the program's non-clinical focus as well as the opportunity it provided to integrate her interests in Women's Studies.

Ms. H identified a number of strengths in the program. First, she feels the skills she has learned in understanding system dynamics, developing multiple perspectives on a problem, grant-writing, research and working collaboratively will help her in her future career. Moreover, she finds the high degree of integration among her classes gives her all the tools she needs to set up, manage and evaluate a program. She also finds faculty members particularly responsive to student needs: [they] "really practice what they preach" and are willing to negotiate changes in classes, procedures, etc., with the students. Because of the extensive networking that faculty have done with local agencies, students have a wide choice of internship possibilities. Given the close attention that the faculty pay to their students, Ms. H felt that they might be "overburdened" and she sometimes felt she was impinging on them.

Mr. Y completed his MA in 1995 and is now attending law school. Before coming to PSH, he earned his bachelor's degree in computer science and worked in that field, but felt "disconnected from the community" and thus decided to get a degree in community psychology.

He was attracted to the program because of its holistic approach to viewing the community and its emphasis on systemic interventions, as opposed to a "band-aid" approach. He also liked that the Master's Paper and the Practicum could be integrated; students could work in a setting and then do applied research relevant to that organization.

Mr. Y. identified the strengths of the program as: (1) the conceptual framework to approach problems from multiple perspectives, (2) the research and evaluation skills, and (3) the grant-writing experience. On the negative side, he felt the program should put less emphasis on mental health issues and, like Ms. H, he thought the program was understaffed.

Sage's Master of Arts program in Community Psychology began in 1980. The goals of the program, as noted in the most recent catalog, are:

1. Reorient the students thinking from a traditional model to newer, more community-oriented models.
2. Train the student in a variety of strategies to facilitate alteration of behavior in community settings.
3. Train the student to evaluate the progress of social service programs.
4. Provide the student with evaluation, assessment and consultation skills.
5. Provide the student with a concentration in counseling, alcohol and drug abuse, child care and children's services or general psychology (The Sage Colleges 1995-96 Catalog, p. 187).

Program Requirements

All students complete 21-24 credits in a core of community psychology and research courses (see Table 2, right column), and then choose additional courses (21-27 credits) from one of four tracks: General Psychology, Chemical Dependency, Child Care and Children's Services or Community Counseling (see Table 3).

All told, students complete 42-51 credits, including an Externship of a minimum of 240 hours in a community agency appropriate for the track. Students must also pass a comprehensive examination and complete a thesis or research seminar.

Faculty

Almost all of the faculty who teach the required courses (Table 2), as well as the courses in the other tracks (Table 3), are full-time members of the Psychology Department.

Students

The Sage Community Psychology program draws most of its students from within a 60 mile radius of the Greater Capitol region (Albany, Schenectady, and Troy, NY). Most students (80% +) are part-time, and courses are scheduled for evenings and weekends. Students typically take 3 to 4 years to complete their degrees. Since the program's inception in 1980, approximately 175 students have earned degrees.

Admission Requirements

All applicants must: (1) have completed a baccalaureate degree from an accredited institution, (2) have a 2.75 GPA or higher (on a 4 point scale) during their junior and senior years, (3) submit Graduate Record Examination Scores (General Test), (4) prepare a statement describing the reason for seeking admission to the program, and (5) provide two letters of reference. While a majority of applicants have degrees in psychology, sociology or related disciplines, applicants from other backgrounds are encouraged to apply (particularly if they have had experience working on planned social change activities), but may be asked to take additional courses to strengthen their background.

STUDENT'S PERSPECTIVE

We interviewed a current student and a recent graduate to get their perspectives on the program at Sage. Ms. H., a part-time student, currently works in a criminal justice agency and deals with youth recidivism. She appreciates the focus of community psychology on evaluation and noted "you need to evaluate the process [for change] not the people."

Ms. H also likes the emphasis on prevention as opposed to treatment and found that the program combined an ecological perspective with a feminist one that was in perfect accord with her own needs. She believes the strength of the program lies in the faculty. Material is presented in a clear and systematic way, and there is strong coordination and integration of concepts between classes. Ms. H feels that she has acquired research, writing and interpersonal skills that will allow her to work in a collaborative way with the public. The opportunity for students to choose externships from a wide range of alternatives (reflecting the integration of Department faculty into local agencies) is another strength of the program.

Ms. P, a recent graduate of the Sage program, chose to pursue community psychology because of her interest in the ways in which change occurs in the system of community services. Ms. P thoroughly enjoyed the program and said that it was "[a] wonderful experience." She particularly enjoyed the small group experiences in her classes and felt that the interactions with her fellow students made the classes more understandable, and more productive, since many had work experience in human services. She further identified strengths of the program as: a nurturing environment, an understanding and cooperative faculty, and its ability to facilitate personal growth.

Conceptually, she liked the multi-level perspective that was presented; she noted: "I liked looking at *all* the stakeholders." Ms. P felt that the skills she developed in the program, e.g., cultural sensitivity, public speaking, conciseness in speaking and writing, active listening and program development and evaluation would be particularly valuable.

DEVELOPING A MASTER'S PROGRAM IN COMMUNITY PSYCHOLOGY

Creating a new graduate program is always a time-consuming and energy-demanding task. Since most of the programs examined are non-doctoral institutions, our comments are focused on this type of institution. Moreover, depending on whether the institution is public or private, different local and state policies may need to be followed. Based on the comments from program directors, we offer the following four guidelines.

1. Develop broad department level support for the proposed program. Although starting a new program may be the initiative of a subset of the department, it is important to involve as many department members as possible in the planning, teaching and administration of the new program. Any new program will inevitably draw resources away from other departmental priorities, and having broad support will minimize the political ramifications of such redirectment. Moreover, you will need all the advocates you can get as your proposal moves beyond the department level! Most academics and university administrators are unfamiliar with community psychology, and any member of your department may be called upon to be an impromptu proponent for the program.

2. Know your market. As community psychologists, we should be particularly attuned to "fitting" in to our local context. What special features of our region help define our likely audiences? Three of the programs examined here are close to their respective state capitals and attract state employees with courses in program evaluation and administrative issues. A program located in a rural area chose to focus on rural community/clinical psychology.

3. Be able to justify the need for your program. In this era of tight budgets, colleagues and university officials will want to know *why* the university should devote resources to your program. Be prepared to document the need for the program. Knowing your market will help you answer such questions as: Who will the program serve? How many students might it draw? Are there similar programs nearby? Proposing a new program may mean downsizing or down-cycling existing programs or courses; be prepared to explain the consequences of these changes. As mentioned earlier, community psychology programs tend not to be big money-makers for universities, but are often an excellent way of getting students (and faculty) into the community which can enhance the reputation of the university as well as help it fulfill its public service mission (particularly if it's a public institution).

4. Identify your resources. Graduate programs tend to be resource intensive, so a thorough review of current department resources is critical. Three key resources are faculty expertise, faculty time and student support. Do enough of your faculty have expertise in the required areas? Good graduate programs can not be built on the backs of one or two faculty. While almost all programs employ some adjunct faculty, there is a strong commitment to maximize the use of full-time faculty to teach the graduate courses.

Graduate programs put heavy demands on faculty time. Establishing and supervising internships, serving on thesis committees, deciding on graduate assistantships/fellowships, developing advertising materials, reviewing student applications are but a few of the additional responsibilities that come when graduate programs are added to undergraduate education. At many institutions, graduate courses carry increased load credit so that faculty teaching these courses may teach fewer courses, shifting more of the burden of undergraduate education to the remaining department faculty. Most master's level universities do not have sufficient numbers of teaching assistantships to offset this shift. The issue of resources is a constant one at most master's level programs and it seems that many programs operate as undermanned settings (Barker & Gump, 1964).

Master's level community psychology programs are demanding to create and maintain. Nevertheless, they provide both faculty and students with exciting opportunities to "make a difference" in their local communities.

NOTE

1. The authors would like to thank Robert Colman, Peter Keller, Michael Morris, Patricia O'Connor and Isaac Prillelpensky for their assistance.

REFERENCES

Barker, R. G., & Gump, P. V. (1964). *Big school, small school: High school size and student behavior.* Stanford, CA: Stanford University Press.

Glazer, J. (1986). *The Master's degree: Tradition, diversity, innovation.* Washington, DC: Association for the Study of Higher Education.

Hoffnung, R. J., Morris, M. M., & Jex, S. (1986). Training community psychologists at the Master's level: A case study of outcomes. *American Journal of Community Psychology, 14,* 339-349.

Kelly, J. G. (1970). Antidotes for ignorance: Training for a community psychology. *American Psychologist, 25,* 524-531.

Rappaport, J. (1981). In praise of paradox: A social policy of empowerment over prevention. *American Journal of Community Psychology, 9,* 1-25.

Silverman, W. H. (1978). Fundamental role characteristics of the community psychologist. *Journal of Community Psychology, 6,* 207-215.

Trent, J. T. (1993). Issues and concerns in master's level training and employment. *Journal of Clinical Psychology, 49,* 586-592.

Doctoral Education in Clinical-Community Psychology

Greg Meissen
Susan Slavich
Wichita State University

SUMMARY. This paper provides an overview of doctoral clinical-community psychology programs and highlights some possible future directions in training. Clinical-community doctoral programs were categorized as: (1) formally labeled clinical-community programs, (2) clinical programs with a formal community track, or (3) clinical programs with an informal community emphasis. Many graduates from these programs obtain a basic understanding and appreciation of community psychology through required or elective courses, and through contact with students and faculty involved in community research and action. Those students who focus their research and electives around community psychology obtain a thorough and in-depth training experience in community research and action. Changes precipitated by managed care will challenge current ways that psychological services are provided allowing for more community based, innovative, and preventive approaches for which community psychology training would be particularly useful. Greater flexibility in APA accreditation guidelines provide opportunities for greater flexibility within clinical-community programs. Doctoral programs in clinical-community psychology are positioned to lead the development of a public health and human service approach to doctoral training through the integration of community and clinical psychology. *[Article copies available for a fee from The Haworth Document Delivery Service: 1-800-342-9678. E-mail address: getinfo@haworth.com]*

[Haworth co-indexing entry note]: "Doctoral Education in Clinical-Community Psychology." Meissen, Greg, and Susan Slavich. Co-published simultaneously in *Journal of Prevention & Intervention in the Community* (The Haworth Press, Inc.) Vol. 15, No. 1, 1997, pp. 31-43; and: *Education in Community Psychology: Models for Graduate and Undergraduate Programs* (ed: Clifford R. O'Donnell, and Joseph R. Ferrari.) The Haworth Press, Inc., 1997, pp. 31-43. Single or multiple copies of this article are available for a fee from The Haworth Document Delivery Service [1-800-342-9678, 9:00 a.m. - 5:00 p.m. (EST). E-mail address: getinfo@haworth.com].

The next decade promises many changes in the education of doctoral psychologists. The implementation of outcome based accreditation procedures by the American Psychological Association (APA) will allow greater flexibility for clinical-community doctoral programs, as well as other clinical programs desiring a stronger community emphasis. Clinical-community programs have historically pressed the limits of the "check-list" accreditation process in an attempt to provide a thorough grounding in community psychology without threatening APA accreditation of their clinical training program. The new accreditation procedures also allow APA approval of doctoral programs beyond just clinical, counseling, and school psychology, such as Industrial/Organizational Psychology, Health Psychology, and Applied Developmental Psychology. The new accreditation guidelines also allow doctoral programs to be accredited as clinical-community programs instead of clinical training programs. Similar flexibility is predicted in the accreditation of internships especially with the current shortage of APA approved internships sites (Murray, 1995; 1996). Finally, changes precipitated by managed care will challenge current ways that psychological services are provided allowing for more community based, innovative, and preventive approaches in which community psychology training would be particularly useful (Humphrey, 1996). This paper provides an overview of current training in doctoral clinical-community programs and attempts to highlight some of these future possibilities.

Historically, clinical-community psychology doctoral programs have developed within existing APA approved clinical training programs. Community psychology has developed as both an alternative to clinical psychology and as an adjunct to or emphasis within clinical psychology. While questioning many of the tenets of clinical psychology, community approaches are also quite attractive to clinical psychology training programs because those approaches hold great promise in developing cost-effective interventions, particularly preventive interventions, that reach much larger numbers of people in natural settings. Clinical-community doctoral programs also provide an academic setting for the continuing development of interventions of this nature through research and action.

At times, the development of clinical-community doctoral programs have been planned, and at other times, an emphasis in community psychology within a clinical training program developed more informally as one or more faculty interested in community research and action became established. The community aspect of most clinical-community programs centers around a small subset of program faculty, typically with formal training in clinical psychology, but deeply interested in community research and action. Interest in community psychology within these programs tends to vary over time as program faculty interested in community psychology increase or decrease in number. Those programs that have more formally established community training within clinical programs (e.g., required community courses of all program students, formal community track) are more stable in providing community training over time, and are less dependent on one or two faculty with strong interest in community research and action.

For purposes of this article, existing clinical-community psychology programs were categorized as either (1) formally labeled clinical-community programs which require community courses of all students in the program, (2) clinical programs with a formal community track that students can select as a minor or emphasis, or (3) clinical programs with an informal community emphasis through the availability of community courses which are not required nor make up a formal track. The programs within the categories described generally and the programs highlighted to provide examples come from the member institutions of the Council of Program Directors in Community Research and Action (CPDCRA), and from the 1995 survey of community psychology graduate programs (Meissen, Slavich, Colgate, Petersan & Dorr, 1995). The report based on the survey of community psychology graduate programs provides more in-depth information about the individual programs discussed in this article (Meissen, Slavich, Colgate, Petersan & Dorr, 1995).

CLINICAL-COMMUNITY PHD PROGRAMS

The graduate programs that were categorized as clinical-community doctoral programs include the University of Illinois at Urbana/Champaign, the University of Maryland at College Park, the University of South Carolina, and Wichita State University. Illinois, Maryland, and South Carolina formally identify themselves as clinical-community programs, and are generally similar in their approach to training in community psychology in that all students in the program are required to enroll in some community psychology courses. Wichita State University, which formally identifies itself as a community-clinical program, is different in its history and training philosophy. A description of the dominant clinical-community approach to training within this category of programs represented by Illinois, Maryland and South Carolina will be outlined, followed by a description of the community-clinical program at Wichita State to provide contrast, and as an example of possible future approaches to integrating community and clinical training.

Interest in community psychology at Maryland, Illinois, and South Carolina historically developed within their existing APA approved clinical training programs. Students in the program take a number of core clinical courses and supervised clinical practica sufficient to compete for APA approved clinical internships, and qualify for licensure as clinical psychologists. One to three community courses are also required of all students insuring a familiarity with community psychology values and basic concepts. There is community psychology related material in other required clinical courses. Students who are specifically interested in community psychology can take additional community psychology courses as electives, and typically engage in practica in community settings.

In addition to course work and practica, students have a number of opportunities for community psychology experience through participation in research teams, typically in community settings which often include a service or action component. Students who pursue these community opportunities gain much experience regarding methodological and intervention issues in community and organizational settings. Collaboration of graduate students with faculty in community research and action, often culminating in their dissertation, is likely to be the most significant community psychology training influence of these programs. There are typically two or three faculty with whom students can collaborate, whose primarily academic identification is community psychology. Some of these students also primarily identify themselves as community psychologists based, in part, on the nature of their pre-doctoral internship, and on the setting in which they are employed after receiving their PhD.

Clinical training in these same programs comes more from the course work and practica which involve a substantially larger number of faculty, who primarily identify themselves as clinical psychologists. A majority of the students in clinical-community programs also do their dissertation research with faculty who identify themselves as clinical psychologists, and upon graduation these students also identify themselves as clinical psychologists. With few exceptions, all students in these programs complete an APA approved clinical internship, though some of the students interested in community psychology are able to find internships that offer significant community related opportunities. In summary, graduates of the formally identified clinical-community doctoral programs secure an understanding and appreciation of community psychology as an adjunct to their clinical training, and some focus their research and electives around community psychology which provides a thorough training experience in community research and action.

In contrast, the community-clinical doctoral program at Wichita State provides a more balanced integration of community and clinical psychology for all students in the program. Much of the philosophical approach to this integration is reflected in Kelly's (1990) encouragement that a union between clinical and community is now possible because of the advances in both fields. A number of community psychologists, along with other applied researchers, have documented the effectiveness of prevention interventions while clinical research has documented the precursors of many problems. Community psychologists also have a history of developing empirically sound, community based interventions in close collaboration with service providers and consumers (Levine, Toro & Perkins, 1993; Tolan, Keys, Chertok & Jason, 1990). These advances allow the design, implementation and evaluation of interventions, especially prevention programs, in community settings based on this theory and research. Kelly (1990, p. 784) argues for "clinical psychology to be practiced as public health." Consequently, there is a dedication to integration with generally equivalent community and clinical requirements rather than having significantly more required clinical courses and practica at Wichita State. The balance in course work and practica is possible because of an approximately equal number of community and clinical faculty. A review of other clinical-community programs shows that with few exceptions, faculty have degrees from APA approved clinical training programs.

Wichita State seeks applicants who have a genuine interest in both community and clinical psychology but do not have a primary interest in becoming licensed clinical psychologists as accreditation will be sought as a community-clinical program. Wichita State's program is a five year full time program which includes a year long, full time pre-doctoral internship. It has proven difficult, and will continue to be difficult, to obtain APA approved clinical internships as students do not possess the quantity of traditional clinical course work and supervised practica compared to students from clinical training programs. Further, most Wichita State students desire internship placements that further both their community and clinical training. Consequently, local internships that reflect an integration of community and clinical psychology are being developed for Wichita State students. Nevertheless, students interviewed believe there would be advantages if these internships were accredited. The intention is to request accreditation of these internships at the same time accreditation is sought as a community-clinical program as they will reflect the program's training philosophy. More detailed information obtained from WSU student interviews was summarized around central themes that emerged during discussions and is presented below.

What types of jobs do students aspire to have? Students in WSU's

Community-Clinical program have a broad range of career interests. Some are interested in academic and research jobs, others are interested in working for human service, health or mental health agencies, and still others are interested in working as consultants or in some role which allows the development of community interventions. Ideally, they would like positions that utilize both their clinical and community training. They indicated that they would desire positions that have more of a public health emphasis, such as prevention, community outreach, community service integration, public education, and cross training with other agencies, as opposed to more individually oriented positions.

What types of internships do they want? Ideally, students desire APA approved internships that also allow them to build upon their community training and their clinical training. The opportunity to gain further experience in program development, evaluation, policy research, etc., within a public health or prevention framework is desired by many. Students are interested in finding internships that will help them develop skills within their own area of professional interest as well (early childhood prevention, depression in the elderly).

Do students worry about getting an internship because of the nature of their training? WSU students are quite concerned about obtaining internships because they are afraid that the blend of community and clinical training they receive will make it difficult for them to be competitive for traditional APA approved internships compared to students' clinical training programs. Students believe the development of local, captured internships that blend community and clinical psychology will provide a better fit for their needs.

Would students take fewer/more clinical courses if that were possible? Most students are happy with the current balance of courses, but wish there were fewer required courses. While none of the students would argue that the number of clinical courses is extensive, some would still desire fewer while others would like more clinical offerings, particularly clinical practice courses.

How do students like combining clinical and community training? Students seem to agree that community and clinical training complement one another. While most students do not believe that clinical training is essential to function as community psychologists, they believe that the clinical skills they acquire are valuable in most aspects of community based work. WSU's students believe that coming from a dual-emphasis program is an advantage, and that it will make them more desirable to prospective employers in the changing health and mental health environment.

How does community and clinical practicum compare? The program at

WSU requires its students to take three semesters each of clinical and community practicum. Many students desire more practicum experience. The community practicum in which they have been involved is more "real world" and provides them with greater responsibility than their clinical practicum. Students often have more opportunity for additional paid community practicum.

Clinical Programs with a Formal Community Track

A number of clinical programs include formal community psychology tracks or emphases including Arizona State, Bowling Green, DePaul, Rutgers, Wayne State, and Loyola University, Chicago. Some of these programs have other tracks that also serve as emphases for clinical graduate students (e.g., child-clinical, health psychology). All of the programs with community tracks are APA approved clinical training programs and students take core clinical courses and practica to qualify for APA approved clinical internships and licensure as clinical psychologists. Students select the community track similarly to students who select a "child" or "health" track as a secondary emphasis within clinical psychology. Students in the community track take additional community psychology courses and can often engage in community practica. Those in the community track, for the most part, collaborate with faculty who identify themselves as community psychologists or have significant activity in community research and action. With few exceptions, all students in these programs complete an APA approved clinical internship, though some of the students interested in community psychology are able to find internships that offer significant community related opportunities. The doctoral program at Arizona State University will be highlighted as an example of a program with a well developed, formal community track with a prevention emphasis.

Community psychology at Arizona State University is an area of emphasis within the clinical psychology program. The clinical training program is based upon a contemporary form of the scientist-practitioner model of professional training, with a strong emphasis on research. In addition to solid academic backgrounds, students are selected for admission on the basis of interest in this approach to clinical psychology. Arizona State's program is designed to be a full-time five year program, including a one-year, full-time internship. The organization of the graduate program allows students to obtain practical clinical training beginning in their second year of graduate school. Student interviews showed that placements in APA approved internships were desired by most of the students in the community track. Many of these students look for internship sites that emphasize research, and provide opportunities for them to use their skills in prevention, working with minority populations, and their experience in community settings. While some students are concerned about obtaining APA placements because their clinical requirements are lower than they have been in the past, this has not proved to be a problem to date as Arizona State has an excellent record of placing students in quality internships. The students in the program find the blend of community and clinical training they receive to be valuable in preparing them for a wide variety of career opportunities. Some students wish they had more flexibility allowing for additional community experience, while some students believe that it would be detrimental if that flexibility came at the expense of fewer clinical requirements.

Course work for students in the community psychology track includes the core clinical curriculum, plus available seminars in community psychology, epidemiology, social support, stress and coping, program evaluation, quasi-experimental design, and community practicum. In addition, many of the clinical placements have some community emphasis. Students in the community track become involved in settings or with populations in which they can utilize skills they have obtained in the program including working with minority populations and being involved in preventive approaches. The students believe that their training in clinical and community psychology provides them with a background that enables them to enhance the effectiveness of their placement site in whatever capacity they work. A majority of Arizona State's graduates from the community track follow scientific or academic careers, but some pursue careers in applied settings.

Besides community psychology course work, students receive a broad range of experience via participation in research teams and community placements. Arizona State has a number of faculty with active research projects in the areas of prevention research and community psychology. For example, students are involved with ongoing projects in the area of minority and cross-cultural mental health. Additionally, there are projects which involve studying risk and protective factors for children of divorce, bereaved children, children of alcoholic families, and inner-city children through the National Institute of Mental Health funded Preventive Intervention Research Center. The Prevention Research Center also provides students with the opportunity to obtain supervised clinical skills in community based settings. Students who pursue the community track have the opportunity to gain considerable experience regarding methodological and intervention issues in community settings, many which have a prevention focus. Active involvement of students in all aspects of research and action is encouraged. Students who were interviewed believed that community training opportunities at Arizona State will increase in the future.

In summary, all students from doctoral programs with formal community tracks have the opportunity to obtain a basic understanding and appreciation of community psychology as an adjunct to their clinical training through electives. Students become aware of community psychology values and approaches even if they do not take community courses through contact with students and faculty involved in community research and action. Those students who select the community track as their emphasis focus their research and electives around community psychology which provides a thorough and in-depth training experience in community research and action. More detailed information obtained from Arizona State (ASU) student interviews was summarized around central themes that emerged during discussions and is presented below.

What types of jobs do students aspire to have? Students in the Community/Prevention track vary in the types of jobs they aspire to have. Many are interested in working in research settings like the Preventive Intervention Research Center. Many also aspire to academic jobs as another setting to be able to conduct research. Some students are interested in work with minorities in either community or more traditional clinical settings while some aspire to work in community based preventive and intervention programs.

What types of internships do they want? ASU students desire APA approved internships, often favoring those with a research emphasis, but that also match their own professional interests and strengths (e.g., minorities, urban setting). ASU students do not necessarily look for community focused internships instead concentrating on acquiring high quality internships in established sites that provide research opportunities.

Do students worry about getting an internship as a result of their type of training? ASU's students worry some about getting internships because the program's clinical requirements are lower than they have been in the past. Nevertheless, ASU has an excellent track record, and getting internships has not become a problem.

Would students take fewer/more clinical courses? The ASU students interviewed believe that their clinical training is critical for the type of work most students will do, and should not be reduced. While some ASU's students might prefer that they did not have so many clinical requirements, others believe that they have a good balance of clinical course work along with other prevention and intervention training.

How do students feel about combining clinical and community training? ASU students believe that they have more employment opportunities coming from a clinical program with a strong community track. They consider their clinical training valuable for the work they want to do and helpful in getting positions that allow that work. Nevertheless, they recognize that students from free standing community programs will have more training and experience in community based research, program evaluation, needs assessment, and other areas attractive to research organizations.

What kind and how much community practicum is done? While ASU does not officially have community practicum, students have the opportunity to take it as an elective. In this practicum, they might be working, for example, in a community agency or facilitating bereaved children's groups. Students may also have a clinical practicum which incorporates some community aspects. But, like their internship sites, students typically are in traditional clinical practicum settings. At the same time, students draw on their training in prevention, community, and working with minority populations in these clinical settings.

Clinical Programs with an Informal Community Emphasis

Clinical programs with an informal community emphasis include the University of Vermont, University of Nebraska, University of California at Berkeley, University of Connecticut, Virginia Tech, and the University of Wyoming. These programs are APA approved clinical training programs and students take core clinical courses and practica to qualify for APA approved clinical internships and licensure as clinical psychologists. Few of the programs require community courses, but students within the clinical program may elect to take available community courses and practica based on their interests. Generally, there are fewer community courses available compared to the programs described above with formal community tracks or with community courses required of all students in the program. In some of these programs, faculty are encouraged to incorporate community psychology values and materials into clinical courses. With few exceptions, all students in these programs complete an APA approved clinical internship, though some of the students interested in community psychology are able to find internships that offer significant community related opportunities.

Most of these programs offer rich community psychology training opportunities through ongoing faculty research and action programs. While a majority of students within these doctoral programs do not obtain significant community psychology training, those students interested in community psychology receive a substantial experience primarily through collaboration with faculty interested in community research and action, often leading to their dissertation research. In summary, all students from these doctoral programs have the opportunity to obtain a basic understanding and appreciation of community psychology as an adjunct to their clinical training through electives. Even those student who do not take community courses become aware of community psychology values and approaches through contact with students and faculty who are engaged in community research and action. The students interested in community psychology focus their research and electives toward the available experiences in community research and action, providing a significant training experience in community psychology.

Future Directions in Training

Over the past two decades training in clinical psychology has gravitated toward two primary approaches. Some doctoral programs, exemplified by professional schools of psychology, are taking a much stronger practitioner approach with the dominant focus on individual treatment. Most of the other clinical training programs are continuing a scientist-practitioner model with much diversity in research but much less diversity in "practice." Changes in accreditation will allow more innovation and diversity in practice for these scientist-practicitioner programs which could include community psychology training emphases such as prevention, needs assessment, program evaluation, policy, and community interventions. An issue that every clinical-community doctoral program faces is the balance of community and clinical course work and practica. The related question of what courses are required of all students or of just some students can be difficult. Both programs highlighted above provide students the opportunity to obtain an academic experience that is relatively balanced between community and clinical training which is consistent with the anticipated flexibility in the new APA accreditation guidelines. The new guidelines should be reassuring to new and existing programs that wish to provide more training in community psychology within clinical psychology programs.

It is anticipated that similar flexibility in the approval of internship sites will follow the flexibility found in the new APA program accreditation guidelines. It has been routinely difficult for clinical students with a strong community interest to find internships which allow much supervised practice of community skills, but prior to this year, students were able to find good clinical internships because of the strength and reputation of their programs. Figures from the Association of Psychology Postdoctoral and Internship Centers (APPIC) Clearinghouse that matches unfilled internship sites and available students show that almost 500 students, primarily from APA approved clinical training programs, did not find internships for the academic year 1996-97. It is important to note that the number of unmatched students reported is an underestimate, as it only reflects those students who chose to participate in the clearinghouse. Almost all of these students will be seeking APA approved internships for 1997-98 year which promises to add to the internship crisis, particularly since no increase in internships is predicted for next year (Murray, 1996). It appears this situation will continue to worsen as the gap between available internship sites and students who need an APA approved internship for program, licensing, or employment requirements will continue to grow. Developing new internships that reflect an integration of community and clinical psychology could address the current internship crisis for students from clinical-community programs.

Managed care is producing major changes in the manner that psychological services are provided (Hayes & Heiby, 1996, Pachman, 1996). Strong trends are already occurring in the preferred use of master's level therapists at the expense of doctoral level clinical psychologists by capitated health maintenance organizations which are quickly becoming the dominant form of managed care (Belar, 1995; Broskowski, 1995). One response to these changes is to increase the medicalization of psychology through prescription and hospital privileges for doctoral level clinical psychologists (DeLeon & Wiggins, 1996). An alternative approach is to follow Kelly's (1990) encouragement for clinical psychology to be practiced as public health by providing psychologists with community psychology skills including a stronger emphases on prevention, consumer responsibility, cost-efficiency of services, outcome evaluation, and use of natural helpers. Humphrey (1996, p. 195) argues that the impending crisis in doctoral level clinical psychology precipitated by managed care actually "reopens the universe of alternatives" for clinical psychology. Instead of focusing doctoral level clinical training on individual treatment, psychologists with community psychology skills can have substantial impacts through program development and evaluation, social policy, and working to develop better ways to help those that populate our institutions, especially our public institutions (e.g., schools, public mental health system). Doctoral programs in clinical-community psychology are positioned to lead in the development of a public health and human service approach to doctoral training through the integration of community and clinical psychology.

REFERENCES

Belar, C. D. (1995). Collaboration in capitated care: Challenges for psychologists. *Professional Psychology: Research and Practice, 26,* 139-146.

Broskowski, A.T. (1995). The evolution of health care: Implications for the training and careers of psychologists. *Professional Psychology: Research and Practice, 26,* 156-162.

DeLeon, P. H. & Wiggins, J. G. (1996). Prescription privileges for psychologists. *American Psychologist, 51,* 225-229.
Kelly, J. G. (1990). Changing contexts and the field of community psychology. *American Journal of Community Psychology, 18,* 769-792.
Hayes, S. C. & Heiby, E. (1996). Psychology's drug problem: Do we need a fix or should we just say no? *American Psychologist, 51,* 198-206.
Humphrey, K. (1996). Clinical psychologists as psychotherapists: History, future & alternatives. *American Psychologist, 51,* 190-197.
Levine, M., Toro, P.A., & Perkins, D. V. (1993). Social and community interventions. *Annual Review of Psychology, 44,* 525-558.
Meissen, G. J., Slavich, S., Colgate, J., Petersan, P., & Dorr, D. (1995). A survey of graduate education in community psychology. *Community Psychologist, 28,* 6-27.
Murray, B. (1995). Are internships getting harder to find? *American Psychological Association Monitor, July,* p. 58.
Murray, B. (1996). Survey sparks call for changes in internships. *American Psychological Association Monitor, April,* p. 48.
Pachman, J. S. (1996). The down of a revolution in mental health. *American Psychologist, 51,* 213-215.
Tolan, P., Keys, C., Chertok, F., & Jason, L. (1990). *Researching community psychology.* Washington, D.C.: American Psychological Association.

Free-Standing Doctoral Programs in Community Psychology: Educational Philosophies and Academic Models

Leah K. Gensheimer
Charles T. Diebold

University of Missouri-Kansas City

SUMMARY. Free-standing community psychology programs (FSCPPs) uniquely train psychologists in non-traditional roles suited to address human and social problems. While the missions of these programs are similar, differences exist in execution. The current status of FSCPPs is presented and key aspects of training are discussed to provide insights for program development. Information was gathered from program documents and interviews with program directors and

---

Address correspondence to Leah K. Gensheimer, University of Missouri-Kansas City, Department of Psychology, 5100 Rockill Road, Kansas City, MO 64110.

The authors thank the free-standing community psychology program directors who graciously endured lengthy telephone interviews and provided descriptive documentation, course outlines, and other program materials and literature: William S. Davidson, James Emshoff, Diane Hughes, Christopher B. Keys, Clifford R. O'Donnell, and Melvin N. Wilson. The authors also thank the students who, endured a grueling telephone interview: Rebecca Campbell, Dale Fryxell, and Cheryl Sutherland. The information obtained from all these individuals made this article possible.

[Haworth co-indexing entry note]: "Free-Standing Doctoral Programs in Community Psychology: Educational Philosophies and Academic Models." Gensheimer, Leah K., and Charles T. Diebold. Co-published simultaneously in *Journal of Prevention & Intervention in the Community* (The Haworth Press, Inc.) Vol. 15, No. 1, 1997, pp. 45-64; and: *Education in Community Psychology: Models for Graduate and Undergraduate Programs* (ed: Clifford R. O'Donnell, and Joseph R. Ferrari) The Haworth Press, Inc., 1997, pp. 45-64. Single or multiple copies of this article are available for a fee from The Haworth Document Delivery Service [1-800-342-9678, 9:00 a.m. - 5:00 p.m. (EST). E-mail address: getinfo@haworth.com].

students. Curriculum issues surrounding course work, field training, research and promoting a multidisciplinary perspective are discussed, and innovative training approaches are highlighted. Two FSCPPs are specifically profiled. Other issues addressed are program resources and the employment of graduates. *[Article copies available for a fee from The Haworth Document Delivery Service: 1-800-342-9678. E-mail address: getinfo@haworth.com]*

Recent writings by academic and clinical psychologists regarding changes in the discipline, the needs of society and the implications of such for the education of future psychologists (e.g., Robiner, 1991; Schneider, 1991) are strikingly reminiscent of discussions held three decades ago which led to the birth of community psychology (Bennett et al., 1966) and prompted the development of alternative educational models, among which included free-standing doctoral programs in community psychology. Free-standing community psychology programs are a prime venue for training a breed of psychologists competent to address pressing problems of the times; psychologists interested in seeking solutions to social problems by adopting an ecological, systems-level approach.

Although other doctoral programs have come to embrace community psychology (e.g., clinical-community, applied social, human development, etc.), free-standing community programs are in a unique position to structure training exclusively on issues relevant to community psychology. Such freedom, however, presents unique challenges for program planning and administration. In this article we identify key aspects of training that warrant consideration and provide a look at how these issues are being addressed by existing programs.

Program information presented was collected in conjunction with activities conducted by the national Council of Directors Program in Community Research and Action. Information was sought from Council membership representing free-standing community psychology programs (FSCPPs). There were nine such programs in 1996 (refer to Table 1). Telephone interviews were conducted with acting directors of seven of these programs and written program materials were provided by six of the directors.[1] In this paper we: (a) describe the current status of FSCPPs, (b) discuss curriculum issues, (c) profile two programs in detail, (d) discuss resource and demand issues, and (e) present excerpts from student interviews on the allure of FSCPPs.

TABLE 1. Directory of Free-Standing Community Psychology PhD Programs: 1995-96 Academic Year

University	Program Name- Year Program Began[a]	Director's Name- Phone #	Mailing Address
Georgia State University (GSU)	Community Psychology Program (1978)	James Emshoff 404-651-2029	Dept. of Psychology University Plaza Atlanta, GA 30303
Michigan State University (MSU)	Ecological-Community Program (1972)	William S. Davidson 517-353-5015	Dept. of Psychology Psych. Research Bldg. East Lansing, MI 48824
New York University (NYU)	Community Psychology Program (1970)	Diane Hughes 212-998-7996	Dept. of Psychology 6 Washington Place New York, NY 10003
University of Hawaii at Manoa (UH)	Community Studies Program (1989)	Clifford R. O'Donnell 808-956-6271	Dept. of Psychology 2430 Campus Road Honolulu, HI 96822
University of Illinois at Chicago (UIC)	Community & Prevention Research (1994)	Christopher B. Keys 312-413-2640	Dept. of Psychology 1007 W. Harrison St. Chicago, IL 60607
University of Missouri-Kansas City (UUKC)	Community Psychology Program (1976)	Leah K. Gensheimer 816-235-1065	Dept. of Psychology 5100 Rockhill Road Kansas City, MO 64110
University of Texas at Austin (UT)	Community Psychology Program (1972)	Marc Lewis 512-471-3393	Dept. of Psychology Mezes Hall Austin, TX 78712
University of Virginia (UV)	Community Psychology & Prevention Research (1976)	Tim D. Wilson[b] 804-924-0674	Dept. of Psychology Gilmer Hall Charlottesville, VA 22903
University of Waikato (UW)	Post-Graduate Programme in Community Psychology (1980)	Neville Robertson 647-838-4466 ext. 8300	Dept. of Psychology Hamilton, Aotearoa/ New Zealand

[a]May be approximate
[b]Interview conducted with Melvin N. Wilson

CURRENT STATUS OF FSCPPS

Table 1 is a directory of the nine FSCPPs which were institutional members of the national Council of Program Directors in Community Research and Action in 1996. Six of these programs emerged during the 1970s, a time when much attention in the field was directed toward exploring alternative training models which would prepare psychologists to take on new roles. The twenty plus years of these programs' existence speak to the viability of FSCPPs.

Programs vary considerably in size and structure. Across all programs, the number of core community faculty ranges from 2 (at UH) to 9 (at UIC) with a median of 4. The average number of affiliated faculty is 8 (range of 2 to 14). Most programs admit between 3 to 5 new students from an average of 35 (range 8 to 43) applicants for admission each year. Four programs currently have a student body between 22-26 students (GSU, MSU, NYU, UMKC), four other programs are considerably smaller with 10 or less students (UH, UIC,[2] UT, UV), and one program has 38 students (UW). An estimate of the total number of active graduate students across all programs during the 1995-96 academic year was 166.

The stated philosophies and mission statements of FSCPPs mirror how we have come to define community psychology. Focus of study is explicitly on the broad range of human and social problems (e.g., substance abuse, violence, environmental conditions, etc.), rather than traditional areas of psychological inquiry. An ecological, problem-oriented research perspective is stressed as illustrated by program descriptions such as "students examine the interplay of community, organizational, group and individual factors" (UIC); and "Students are expected and encouraged to think critically about current social issues [and] generate social solutions . . . " (NYU). All programs adopt a scientist-professional model. An empirical approach to social intervention is stressed and all programs emphasize education in basic and applied research methods. Focus is on field research, prevention, and developing and evaluating social intervention strategies.

While the missions of these programs are similar, differences exist in how programs are executed. Unique approaches include a multidisciplinary program of study (UH), adopting an apprenticeship training model (UH, NYU), and an explicit intent to produce "scholar-activists" (MSU). Further variations are discussed in the sections which follow.

CURRICULUM

The curriculum among FSCPPs typically consists of four emphasis areas: course work, field training, research, and a set of elective courses within psychology and/or outside the discipline that promote a multidisciplinary perspective.

Course Work

Is there a "core" of community psychology courses? This is a basic yet very valid question to ask. The foundation of all graduate programs is in-depth course work in the particular discipline or subdiscipline. All programs offer at least one course of introduction to the field, grounding students in community psychology's history, values, theories, research, and strategies, and most also offer an advanced seminar in the field. Other topics commonly considered within the "community core" are courses in community intervention and program evaluation. Beyond these courses, however, what constitutes a program's community core varies greatly. We found it interesting that prevention and empowerment, which have been cited as goals of our field (Shinn, 1987), were not a standard part of curricula. Only two programs required course work in prevention (UIC, UMKC), and two offered empowerment as an elective topic (MSU, UIC). Walfish, Polifka and Stenmark (1984) commented on the deficiency of training in these areas over a decade ago, and apparently improvement is still warranted.

Typically course offerings are contingent upon faculty interests and expertise. A critical mass of faculty with diverse backgrounds is important to ensure students' exposure to a broad range of content areas. Programs with a small number of core faculty can augment instruction by establishing an involved group of affiliated faculty and by establishing collaborative arrangements with colleagues in other departments.

How much foundational course work in general psychology is necessary? APA accredited programs require students to complete breadth course work in general psychology, covering five content areas: the biological bases of behavior, cognitive-affective bases, social bases, individual differences, and scientific methods. This is not the case for FSCPPs. Programs vary substantially in the amount of their curricula devoted to foundational psychology courses, from those requiring only two courses (MSU, NYU, UH) to one requiring six (UMKC). The basic issue is how important is it for program graduates to be able to identify with the traditional discipline. The answer should tie back to a program's mission statement, which calls attention to the importance of establishing well thought out program objectives at the start. Since the "institutional home" (Trickett, Irving, & Perl, 1984) of FSCPPs is within departments of psychology, there are likely to be ardent opinions among faculty on this issue.

What are the standards of professional competence? Despite our stated values of diversity and innovation, there is little innovation in the standards by which we evaluate and judge professional competence among doctoral students in community psychology. All programs adhere to the conventional yardsticks of success: course work performance, thesis, comprehensive examination, and dissertation. If anything has changed over the years, it is an even greater emphasis on traditional measures of achievement. For instance, publication expectations of the graduating student has come to match closely that once held of a tenured-track assistant professor. As raised by leaders in the field over 25 year ago (e.g., Kelly, 1970; Tornatsky, Fairweather, & O'Kelly, 1970), we question the validity of such measures for assessing competence as a social change agent or the numerous other non-academic roles of a community psychologist.

Some degree of innovation does exists. For instance, in two programs (NYU, UV) the thesis requirement involves an empirical piece of research written in a publishable format rather than the conventional style resembling the dissertation. Alternative comprehensive examination requirements were also noted. They range from the more traditional written timed tests (GSU, UMKC) or essay papers (UH) on specific content areas defined by the program, to scholarly theme pieces involving the critical assessment of theory and research on a topic chosen by the student (NYU, UIC). Two programs offer a range of examination options to the student (MSU, UV). The program at MSU, for example, offers five options: written test, scholarly review paper, grant application, develop and teach an undergraduate course, or some other alternative agreed upon by the student's guidance committee.

NYU best exemplifies the integration of alternative educational standards into its curriculum. All program requirements are modeled after professional activities (New York University, 1995): the master's thesis is an empirical piece, written in the form of a journal article, not exceeding 25 double spaced pages; the comprehensive examination involves an article length literature review appropriate for publication in journals like *Psychological Bulletin* or *Psychological Review*, and a policy influence piece designed to promote change in an applied setting; and the dissertation proposal is modeled after a public health service grant proposal, with the final manuscript written in the form of a journal article. Although such requirements counter tradition on one level, they are still very "product" focused. Program directors must be careful not to lose sight of the importance of the "process" of graduate education in promoting innovation and creativity (Rappaport, 1977), attributes so germane to our work in the community.

How structured should curriculum be? The importance of flexibility in curriculum is critical for FSCPPs if they are to achieve their mission of training psychologists for such diverse roles as social change agents, consultants, researchers, evaluators, program developers, administrators, advocates, policy analysts, and professors. Programs can accomplish this by: (a) limiting the number of required courses, allowing sufficient room for elective work in areas relevant to students' interests; (b) placing importance on field training and monitoring for breadth of experiences; (c) adopting alternative measures of scholarship as discussed above; and (d) supporting student independent research.

How do programs ensure timely academic progress of students? Across the FSCPPs contacted, it takes students an average of six years to complete their degrees. While this figure is substantially lower than the 10.4 years reported for all areas of psychology (National Center for Education Statistics, 1995) it is considerably longer than the standard four year curriculum outlined in program descriptions. Why? In most programs, students are expected to be "out in the community" throughout their training. Frequently such community involvement presents students with competing and often more pressing demands than their academic responsibilities. Further, adopting a participant-conceptualizer role and the complexities of conducting community research simply takes time. Students engaged in their own independent community research will take longer than students engaged in laboratory or college-based studies.

Curriculum arrangements and requirements can facilitate students' timely completion of their programs. For instance, at UV and NYU the curricula are structured such that all course work can be completed within three years. This arrangement recognizes the year or more needed for students to devote to their independent research. Other programs have imposed structure at times when students' academic progress typically slows; that is when they are engaged in their own independent work such as doing thesis research or preparing for the comprehensive examination. For instance, NYU requires students who have not completed their thesis to attend a research seminar designed to assist them in the process. At UIC, third year students are required to enroll in a one year independent study course while they work on their comprehensive examination, and established dates exist for submission of related examination materials.

Field Training

Field training is a standard part of doctoral education in community psychology. It provides students with experiences that cannot be approximated in the classroom, but are essential for professional development. In general, field training provides students with opportunities to understand the application of abstract bodies of knowledge (Morell, 1984), gain experience working in natural settings, refine skills, and gain an in-depth understanding of social problems within an ecological context. Further, field training often initiates students to dealing with the ambiguous roles and professional identity issues characterized by the field.

Unlike students in clinical-community programs whose practica options are likely to be restricted by APA requirements and/or their needing to choose placements that will put them in a good position to compete for favored internships (Tolan, 1990), students in FSCPPs have much more freedom in selecting sites and in designing the nature of their experiences. Both traditional (e.g., community mental health centers, social service agencies) and non-traditional settings (e.g., active involvement with a community organizing effort; working to establish coalitions centered around children services) are viable options. Typically it is the non-traditional setting that allows for broader experiences and greater opportunities for students to refine their defining areas of competence. Often students are plunged into roles or given responsibilities comparable to those they will assume when employed after they have earned their degrees.

Field training sites most often used by students among the FSCPPs we contacted were: government agencies, research institutes, advocacy organizations, self-help agencies, women's centers, public health facilities, criminal justice facilities, and schools. Quality field training was characterized by FSCPP directors as: challenging students' knowledge and skills, offering opportunities to take on new responsibilities, compatible with the field's values and methods, providing a diversity of experiences, matching student interests, providing opportunities to observe the process of social change, and providing a broad view of social problems and how organizations and/or communities address them.

The extent of formality of the field training requirement varies across programs. For example, MSU requires students to enroll in only one semester of practicum, although students are involved in field work throughout their participation in the program (W. S. Davidson, personal communication, January 30, 1996); while at UMKC students formally register for practica for four semesters. Procedural aspects of field training noted among programs are: (a) student selects the site with some faculty assistance based on the student's interests; (b) there are no formal administrative agreements established between the graduate program and training sites, but some contract or administrative agreement is established between student and graduate program outlining the nature of training experiences anticipated; (c) supervision is provided by program faculty rather than a site supervisor, either in the context of a class with faculty and peer feedback, or through individual student-faculty supervision arrangement; and (d) some sites financially compensate students for their work. Concern with this latter issue was raised by Rappaport (1977). When students enter a "fee-for-service" arrangement they become employees rather than social change agents and are more vulnerable to organizational pressures. Further, many grass-roots organizations, which could provide students with unique learning experiences, simply can not afford to hire additional persons.

Research

Developing research competence is at the core of all FSCPPs. Research is fundamental to community psychology's approach to understanding and searching for solutions to critical social problems. The complexities and challenges posed by community research, however, demands educational approaches that extend beyond the standard course work in methodology and statistics, or the thesis and dissertation requirements. "Socialization" in the research process is required.

Most FSCPPs set clear expectations for research involvement from the beginning. For instance, NYU strongly conveys this message in their program description: ". . . faculty expect students to be involved in research at least half-time (20 hours per week) throughout their graduate careers" (New York University, 1994, p. 5). UIC gives research involvement formal status by requiring students to enroll in two semesters of research apprenticeship and to attend the research group of at least one faculty member. UH formalizes research by requiring students to be enrolled in directed community research, thesis, or dissertation each semester until completion of the program. Other strategies to socialize students to community research include topical brown bag lunches (UIC, UV) and adopting a formal apprenticeship educational model (NYU, UH).

Promoting a Multidisciplinary Perspective

It is universally accepted that a multidisciplinary perspective is required to gain a comprehensive understanding of complex social problems and to be in a position to propose innovations that hold promise for addressing them. The challenge is how to socialize students to not merely recognize the value of this perspective, but to adopt an approach of routinely collaborating with professionals from various fields. The standard method is to build room into the curriculum for students to take course work in another discipline. Program directors indicated that they encouraged students to take courses from other departments and have the flexibility in their programs to allow for this; however, only two programs *require* such course work (MSU, UH). Other common mechanisms are to invite faculty from other departments to be affiliated with the program and through students' practica.

Some unique measures to promote multidiscipline education were noted among several FSCPPs. For instance, a commitment to a multidiscipline program of study was the foundation upon which the Community Studies Program at UH was built (O'Donnell, 1994). The program incorporates offerings from other departments within the core community curriculum, not just as recommended electives. UIC has capitalized on the resources within the Chicago area to accomplish a multidiscipline education. They have established formal linkages for student course work and collaborative interdisciplinary projects among divisions within the university, other universities within the area, and local organizations.

Course work alone, however, is not likely to be sufficient (Kelly, 1970). Program directors would be wise to broaden further the concept of multidiscipline education by devising creative ways to draw on experts from the community who may, or may not, have the traditional academic credentials but who could greatly contribute to students' understanding of the community. An example of this can be found at NYU. An expert, outside academia, serves as one of the reviewers who evaluates the policy influence piece of a student's comprehensive examination.

PROFILE OF TWO FSCPPS

To further illustrate the variation among FSCPPs we have elected to highlight two programs (see Table 2) which differ substantially in their histories, size, and curriculum: the Ecological-Community Psychology Program at Michigan State University and the Community Studies Program at the University of Hawaii at Manoa.

Ecological-Community Psychology Program at Michigan State University

MSU's program is one of the longest standing and largest FSCPPs. The first degree was awarded in 1972 and since then over 65 PhD degrees have been granted. The current number of core faculty is seven and affiliated

TABLE 2. Program Profile: Michigan State University and University of Hawaii at Manoa

Michigan State University		University of Hawaii at Manoa
	Date Program Began	
1972		1989
	Faculty Profile	
7	Community Core Faculty	2
9	Affiliated Faculty	2
16	Total Faculty	4
	Faculty Interests	
Social change domains, organizational and community development, collaboration, domestic violence, stress and burnout in helping organizations, stress and coping, social supports, homelessness.		Behavior ecology, crime settings, social networks, cultural compatibility programs for at-risk youth, organizational change, institutional climate, social policy planning, community development, activity settings.
	Student Profile	
26	Total # of Students in Program	9
35	Avg. # of Applicants per year	8
5	Avg. # Admitted per year	2
	Philosophy & Mission	
The Ecological-Community Psychology Program has been designed to bring humanitarian and scientific thought to bear upon the solution of critical human problems. The intent of the program is to produce scholar-activists who can carry out socially relevant experiments aimed at solving human problems in their natural setting.		Professional activities are guided by research and databased assessment and directed toward social contexts and settings for the prevention of human problems and the enhancement of social competence. As scientist-practitioners we seek to advance knowledge and influence social policy through research and the application of social intervention strategies.

TABLE 2 (continued)

	Michigan State University	University of Hawaii at Manoa
Multidiscipline Education	As cognate option Dual-degree option: Urban Studies Affiliated Faculty: Criminal Justice, Sociology, Anthropology	In core curriculum Dual-degree option: Urban & Regional Planning; Juris Doctor Affiliated Faculty: Urban & Regional Planning, Education Comp exam on another discipline
Research Emphasis	Ouantitative emphasis (3 required courses) Thesis Dissertation	Qualitative emphasis (2 required courses) Thesis Comp exam requires qualitative analysis essay Dissertation
Measures of Competence	(1) Traditional Masters Thesis (2) Comprehensive Examination: Student defined format and content Coverage areas: history & systems, theory, social change strategies, knowledge of existing research, design, assessment, ethics, future directions, implications. Format Options: Written test review paper, grant application, design and teach undergraduate course, other format by arrangement. (3) Traditional Dissertation	(1) Traditional Masters Thesis (2) Comprehensive Examination: Program defined format and content Coverage areas: community psychology, student's minor, qualitative analysis, dissertation topic Format: Written exam in community psychology Written exam in minor Paper applying qualitative analysis to a specific research problem Oral exam focused on dissertation proposal (3) Traditional Dissertation

faculty is nine. The program admits an average of five new students a year from a pool of about 35 applicants. There were 26 active students in the program during the 1995-96 academic year.

An account of the program's origin is provided by Tornatzky et al. (1970). As that article highlights, the program was a direct outgrowth of the 1960s' concern over pressing social problems and our field's call for a new breed of psychologists whose primary interests were in seeking solutions to these problems and enhancing the general welfare. The program has held to this tradition as illustrated by its current mission statement (refer to Table 2) and by the dissertation topics of graduates over the years, many of which have focused on field experimentation of social interventions. Unique to this program is its heavy emphasis on developing students' competencies in quantitative methods and its adherence to the Experimental Social Innovation and Dissemination Model (Fairweather & Davidson, 1986) of social change. The program provides opportunity for multidiscipline education through course work culminating in a formal minor or cognate area of study in a psychology subdiscipline, another academic discipline, or theme area (e.g., youth issues, measurement).

Community Studies Program at the University of Hawaii at Manoa

In contrast to MSUs program, the community program at UH is newer and smaller. An historical account of the program was provided by O'Donnell (1994). As O'Donnell describes, the program was formally established as a free-standing community psychology program in 1989, when faculty resisted pressure from the professional community to minimize the, then, clinical/community program's community emphasis. Rather than give up the conceptual foundation upon which the program was built, faculty chose to begin a new program.

Today, the program has two core and two affiliated faculty, and admits an average of two new students from about eight applicants a year. By intent, the program is kept small in order to accommodate the educational needs of students. Three unique aspects of the program are its commitment to a multidiscipline program of study, emphasis on qualitative research, and an apprenticeship educational model.

At the core of the program is its commitment to multidiscipline education which is accomplished through several means. First, the program offers dual degree options in either urban and regional planning (MURP-PhD) or law (JD-PhD). Second, course work from other disciplines is incorporated within the core community curriculum. Third, students are required to complete at least three graduate courses in another discipline and pass a minor comprehensive examination focused on that discipline.

Fourth, applications for admissions to the program are sought from persons with diverse educational backgrounds (e.g., majored in public health, political science, communications, etc.), not only those who have majored in psychology.

Another distinguishing feature of UH's program is its emphasis in qualitative research. This is done through required course work in qualitative methods, and by including a qualitative analysis exercise as part of students' comprehensive examination requirement. Course work in quantitative methods is recommended but only one course is required. UH further emphasises the importance of research by formalizing it into course work that is required each semester.

PROGRAM RESOURCES AND PROGRAM DEMAND

We can not have an article focused on program development without commenting on two issues: (a) What resources are necessary, and (b) is there a demand for the program, specifically is there interest among prospective graduate students and are graduates employable?

Program Resources

At the core of a quality community program are "good committed faculty" and "bright hard working students" (C. Keys, personal communication, January 25, 1996). While obvious, the importance of involved faculty for graduate education can not be overstated. Faculty do more than simply teach courses. They are instrumental in the professional socialization of the future leaders in the field. A general consensus is that a minimum of three core community faculty is necessary to support a doctoral program in community psychology in order to ensure students' exposure to a breadth of academic areas and to attract a diversity of program applicants. Further, a low faculty-student ratio is important to ensure sufficient guidance for student independent scholarship.

Another critical resource is financial support for students. Doctoral education in community psychology is a full-time endeavor. Students who must work outside the university setting while pursuing their education are likely to take substantially longer to complete their degrees, have less time to spend in the community engaged in social change activities, and miss out on important professional opportunities and socialization. Common sources for student stipends are departmental teaching assistantships, fellowships, and faculty grants and contracts. The latter source is critical. A program's ability to secure external funding is an indication of a program's strength and contributes to its sustainability by not having to rely on university funds, which are likely to be susceptible to budgetary changes. Further, it is through such faculty activities that students learn the art of negotiation, how to secure funding, the intricacies of community research, and the challenge of balancing theory, research, and action.

Program Demand

Applicants. Arguably, the number of yearly admission applications to FSCPPs is small compared with those for such doctoral programs as clinical, counseling or industrial-organizational psychology (Norcross, Hanych, & Terranova, 1996). This index often is used by universities to justify the "need of a program" when establishing academic priorities. This is unfortunate because it does not take into consideration the valuable services FSCPPs often provide in meeting the needs of the community in which the university is a part. We believe the low number of applicants to FSCPPs is not so much a lack of interest in the field, but rather a lack of basic knowledge of community psychology among prospective graduate students. Although it is doubtful that our numbers will ever reach those comparable to APA accredited programs, more interest in FSCPPs would exist if greater efforts were taken to educate potential students about the field and the career options available.

Are community psychology graduates employable? Probably the single most commonly raised concern by people within and outside our field is the problem of employability. We believe the "problem" is actually a strength due to the diversity of employment positions and settings for those well trained in action research, methodology, program evaluation, prevention and systems and ecological theories. It is simply hard for people to grasp the idea that there is no single answer to the question of "where will graduates find employment?" What Iscoe (1984) stated a decade ago holds true today: "The overall sophistication of community psychology students in research, evaluation, theory and problem-solving makes them attractive to a number of agencies, many of whom have never employed this type of combination of skills" (p. 183).

Studies consistently have found that community psychology graduates have little difficulty finding employment, and secure positions in government, academia, applied research, and evaluation (Feis, Mavis, Weth, & Davidson, 1990; Maton, Meissen, & O'Connor, 1993; Walfish, Polifka, & Stenmark, 1986). Such findings were supported by information we obtained from the directors of FSCPPs.

As we see it, the real problem is convincing others that employment is a *non*-issue. This becomes a challenge because we can not simply turn to job listings for instant validation, since rarely does one see "community psychologist" advertised. The title is not well recognized by the public or even by colleagues in our own discipline. Yet positions are out there, and the 21st century will bring even more possibilities as attention is turned to program accountability, broader community-level interventions, prevention, and health promotion. Graduates need only to identify their "niche" or ecological fit between their competence and interests and employment settings and job types.

From a program management point of view, our challenge is to recognize the concerns around employment and prepare students for ambiguity right from the start. Students need to be made aware of the fact that there are not well established or "institutionalized" career tracks for those trained exclusively in community psychology. Consequently, it is important that students identify desired career paths early in their education so that they can establish a plan of study which will afford them a good job-fit when they complete their degrees. For the most part, the unique nature of the curricula of FSCPPs allows for this thorough encouraging course work in other disciplines, providing a breadth of field training experiences, and emphasizing methodology and applied research.

As a summary, Table 3 outlines some important considerations for those interested in developing, administering and sustaining an FSCPP. The list is based on ideas discussed in this article and those suggested by Program Directors during our interview.

THE ALLURE OF A FREE-STANDING COMMUNITY PSYCHOLOGY PROGRAM: THE STUDENT PERSPECTIVE

We conclude this paper by presenting the perspectives of graduate students on FSCPPs. As noted by these students' comments, despite apparent qualitative differences in programs' training approach and emphasis, the underlying philosophy of the field binds these programs producing psychologists of like vision.

Telephone interviews were conducted with Dale Fryxell from UH, and with Cheryl Sutherland and Rebecca Campbell from MSU. Dale learned of the Community Studies Program while working with the Peace Corps' "Save The Children" initiative. He is pursuing the dual-degree option in community psychology and urban and regional planning (MURP-PhD) to complement his interests in prevention and public policy. Dale currently coordinates the Positive Behavior Supports Project which studies environmental factors that affect people with developmental disabilities. Cheryl

TABLE 3. Considerations for Developing, Administering and Sustaining a FSCPP

1. Mobilize and sustain a critical mass of quality faculty (min. 3 full-time core faculty) who have diverse interests, are committed to the values of community psychology, are involved in ongoing research, and have external research support.
2. Establish a group of involved affiliated faculty with varied expertise from diverse disciplines, and develop collaborative arrangements with other university departments or divisions for course offerings and dual degree options.
3. Formulate a clear, objective mission statement which identifies the type of graduates produced by the program and guides program activities.
4. Obtain department support and commitment to the program.
5. Secure in-house student financial support (e.g., teaching assistantships, fellowships).
6. Develop curriculum, making decisions about: core community course work, required foundational breadth in psychology, choice of multidiscipline educational strategy (e.g.,) minor, cognate, dual-degree options, involvement of community experts), and innovative measures of professional competence.
7. Establish student research expectations and structure research experiences (e.g., formal apprenticeship model, course work, seminars, independent scholarship).
8. Develop program promotional materials (e.g., brochures) and venues for distribution.
9. Implement aggressive recruitment strategies to attract competitive students who are committed to the values of the field.
10. Establish relationships with the community for collaboration in the areas of research, practica, consultation, etc.
11. Network with others in the field via conferences, internet, etc.
12. Strive for cultural diversity in faculty and students and address diversity issues in curriculum.

Sutherland had worked as a recreation supervisor at a residential facility for adjudicated boys prior to graduate work. The recidivism rates among these youth was disconcerting to her and the facility's ideology did not match her own. At MSU, Cheryl became interested in women's health issues, especially domestic violence. She currently directs the Women's Health Project which studies the effect of stressful life circumstances on physical and psychological health. Rebecca Campbell entered MSUs program wanting to learn how to do research in a community setting. She specialized in quantitative methods. While a graduate student she served on several community boards involved with planning local policies and programs addressing violence against women. Rebecca completed her doctorate in May 1996 and has accepted a tenured-track faculty position at the University of Illinois at Chicago. Two common themes emerged from the interviews: identification with the field's ideology and values, and the importance of a multidisciplinary perspective.

The ideology of the field was the primary allure mentioned among the interviewees for selecting community psychology as their choice of graduate study. Dale chose a community psychology program because of its emphasis on prevention and because of its multidisciplinary approach. "Community psychology matched up most closely with what I wanted to do. . . . I was interested in developing prevention programs. . . . and community psychology's multidisciplinary approach was very important because if you are going to be doing comprehensive program development you need to know where the other disciplines are coming from and where their strengths and weaknesses might be" (D. Fryxell, personal communication, May 29, 1996). Rebecca chose the field because she "wanted to be a community psychologist . . . I wanted to learn how to do research in a community setting . . . I wanted to learn how to implement and evaluate community programs" (R. Campbell, personal communication, April 10, 1996). Cheryl valued community psychology not only for its focus on community level work but also for its emphasis on "being out in the community," that is, practicing the philosophy. She also thought it absolutely essential to gain multiple perspectives, including both academic research approaches and the perspectives of the front-line community workers, in order to gain a better understanding of an issue (C. Sutherland, personal communication, April 4, 1996).

Why an FSCPP over other graduate training options in community psychology? The common consensus was that a free-standing program better accommodated the actualization of community psychology theory and practice. "The ideology is filtered throughout . . . it is the core aspect, not ancillary as in a clinical program" (C. Sutherland). "Even the strongest clinical/community program that I know of does not train one thoroughly in community psychology and ultimately pulls you back to an individual level of analysis" (R. Campbell). Furthermore, "in a clinical program you have to spend so much time looking at treatment issues that prevention aspects get lost" (D. Fryxell). In short, "with hybrid programs you are torn between two different ideologies that can create conflict. . . . for me, it is hard to mix different value systems" (C. Sutherland).

NOTES

1. Our data collection procedures were not designed with methodological rigor in mind. The intent was to collect descriptive information about these programs which could be disseminated to others interested in developing similar programs and/or to those interested in knowing how others are "doing it."

2. The program at UIC is new, admitting its first class in the Fall of 1994. It is expected that the number of students in this program will increase over time.

REFERENCES

Bennett, C. C., Anderson, L. S., Cooper, S., Hassol, L., Klein, D. C., & Rosenblum, G. (Eds.). (1966). *Community psychology: A report of the Boston conference on the education of psychologists for community mental health.* Boston: Boston University Press.

Fairweather, G. W., & Davidson, W. (1986). *Community experimentation: Theory, methods, and practice.* New York: McGraw Hill.

Feis, C. L., Mavis, B. E., Weth, J. E, & Davidson, W. S. (1990). Graduate training and employment experiences of community psychologists. *Professional Psychology Research and Practice, 21,* 94-98.

Iscoe, I. (1984). Austin–A decade later: Preparing community psychology students for work in social policy areas. *American Journal of Community Psychology, 12,* 175-184.

Kelly, J. G. (1970). Antidotes for arrogance: Training for community psychology. *American Psychologist, 25,* 524-531.

Maton, K. I., Meissen, G., & O'Connor, P. (1993, Summer). The varying faces of graduate education in community psychology: Comparisons by program type and program level. *The Community Psychologist, 26*(3), 19-21.

Morell, J. A. (1984). Making evaluation viable: The response of graduate programs in evaluation. *American Journal of Community Psychology, 12,* 209-216.

National Center for Education Statistics. (1995). *Digest of education statistics 1995.* (NCES 95-029). Washington, DC: U.S. Department of Education Office of Educational Research and Improvement.

New York University. (1994). *Community psychology doctoral curriculum.* New York: Author.

Norcross, J. C., Hanych, J. M., & Terranova, R. D. (1996). Graduate study in psychology: 1992-1993. *American Psychologist, 51,* 631-643.

O'Donnell, C. R. (1994, Spring). Community studies: A multi-disciplinary program. *The Community Psychologist, 27*(2), 8-10.

Rappaport, J. (1977). Training for a community psychology: Professional and nonprofessional. *Community psychology: Values, research, and action.* (pp. 372-409). New York: Holt, Rinehart & Winston.

Robiner, W. N. (1991). Dialogue on a human resource agenda for psychology: A welcome and a response. *Professional Psychology Research and Practice, 22,* 461-463.

Schneider, S. F. (1991). No fluoride in our future. *Professional Psychology Research and Practice, 22,* 456-460.

Shinn, M. (1987). Expanding community psychology's domain. *American Journal of Community Psychology, 15,* 555-574.

Tolan, P. (1990, Summer). Research training at DePaul University. *The Community Psychologist, 23*(3), 21-22.

Tornatzky, L. G., Fairweather, G. W., & O'Kelly, L. I. (1970). Psychology in action: A PhD program aimed at survival. *American Psychologist, 25,* 884-888.

Trickett, E. J., Irving, J. B., Perl, H. I. (1984). Curriculum issues in community psychology: The ecology of program development and the socialization of students. *American Journal of Community Psychology, 12,* 141-155.

Walfish, S., Polifka, J. A., Stenmark, D. E. (1984). An evaluation of skill acquisition in community psychology training. *American Journal of Community Psychology, 12,* 165-174.

Walfish, S., Polifka, J. A., Stenmark, D. E. (1986). The job search in community psychology: A survey of recent graduates. *American Journal of Community Psychology, 14,* 237-240.

Interdisciplinary Programs in Community and Applied Research

Arthur J. Reynolds

University of Wisconsin-Madison

SUMMARY. This article describes the critical role of interdisciplinary programs in addressing the mission of the Society for Community Research and Action. In the past decade, interdisciplinary approaches to graduate education have increased in importance yet the makeup of the Society does not reflect this change. The mission, organization, and curriculum focus of five programs are described. They include human development and family studies, social welfare, law/psychology, and community-social psychology. Prevention research and program evaluation are highlighted as key areas for program development. *[Article copies available for a fee from The Haworth Document Delivery Service: 1-800-342-9678. E-mail address: getinfo@haworth.com]*

The Society is devoted to advancing theory, research and social action to promote positive well-being, increase empowerment, and prevent the development of problems in communities, groups, and

---

Address correspondence to Arthur J. Reynolds, 1350 University Avenue, University of Wisconsin, Madison, WI 53706.

The author thanks the program chairs at the University of Wisconsin-Madison, University of Nebraska, University of Maryland-Baltimore, and Pennsylvania State University for detailed program information. The author also thanks Stephen Small for helpful suggestions on an earlier version of this paper.

[Haworth co-indexing entry note]: "Interdisciplinary Programs in Community and Applied Research." Reynolds, Arthur J. Co-published simultaneously in *Journal of Prevention & Intervention in the Community* (The Haworth Press, Inc.) Vol. 15, No. 1, 1997, pp. 65-82; and: *Education in Community Psychology: Models for Graduate and Undergraduate Programs* (ed: Clifford R. O'Donnell, and Joseph R. Ferrari.) The Haworth Press, Inc., 1997, pp. 65-82. Single or multiple copies of this article are available for a fee from The Haworth Document Delivery Service [1-800-342-9678, 9:00 a.m. - 5:00 p.m. (EST). E-mail address: getinfo@haworth.com].

> individuals. The action and research agenda of the field is guided by three broad principles. Community research and action is the active collaboration between researchers, practitioners, and community members and utilizes multiple methodologies. Human competencies and problems are best understood by viewing people within their social, cultural, and historical contexts. Change strategies are needed at both the individual and systems levels for effective competence promotion and problem prevention. (Society for Community Research and Action, American Psychological Association)

An important fact about this mission statement from the Society for Community Research and Action of the American Psychological Association is that the discipline of psychology is not mentioned. This was intentional because the creators of Division 27 were interested in fostering interdisciplinary inquiry among social and behavioral science disciplines in the service of redressing social problems and promoting healthy development. While this goal is laudable, interdisciplinary and multidisciplinary practices are not yet a reality. The vast majority of divisional members are psychologists, and nearly all member programs of the training council associated with the division are psychology departments.

The purpose of this chapter is to highlight the role of interdisciplinary programs in addressing the mission of the Society as well as community and applied research generally. Five interdisciplinary doctoral training programs are described in detail. These graduate programs participate in the Council of Program Directors in Community Research and Action (recently changed from Council of Community Psychology Program Directors), which advises the Society on graduate education.

TRENDS IN INTERDISCIPLINARY TRAINING

In the past decade, several trends have reinforced the importance of interdisciplinary training in community research and associated fields that have direct implications for graduate training across the social and behavioral sciences. Three are especially important:

- In 1994, the National Science Foundation initiated the Human Capital Initiative for research opportunities among the social, behavioral and economic sciences to "create a strategic plan for basic research in human capital that encompassed the perspectives of the entire social and behavioral science community" (APS Observer, p. 40). This mission-based initiative identified six major social contexts that affect development and utilization of human capital for research and intervention efforts: Workplace, education, families, neighborhoods, disadvantage, and poverty.

- Prevention research has developed as a field of scientific inquiry and emphasizes several research principles that benefit from collaborative and interdisciplinary research and action (e.g., Coie et al., 1993). These may include the investigation of causal processes of development, transactions between individuals and their environments, program development and evaluation, and knowledge transfer. Training in applied developmental psychology also offers such an approach (Fisher et al., 1993) as do the fields of educational psychology, social work, and the health sciences.
- In the past few years, professional associations have formed that are devoted to major issues of interest to community and applied social research. These include the Association of Applied and Preventive Psychology and the Society for Research on Adolescence. Moreover, professional associations such as the American Evaluation Association, the American Educational Research Association, the National Council on Family Relations, and the Society for Research on Child Development also have much in common with community-related research and graduate training. For example, *Child Development*, the major journal of the Society for Research on Child Development, has initiated a new section devoted to the domain of applied research, program evaluation, and policy studies (Bornstein, 1995).

Interdisciplinary Training in Community Psychology and Associated Programs

The five interdisciplinary doctoral training programs in the Council of Program Directors cover in Community Research and Action a wide variety of research domains from basic research on developmental processes to evaluating social programs and disseminating knowledge about them. These programs are shown in Table 1 and include the Psychology/Law Program at the University of Nebraska, the community-social program in Human Services Psychology at the University of Maryland at Baltimore, two human development and family studies programs (Penn State and University of Wisconsin-Madison), and the Social Welfare Program at the University of Wisconsin at Madison. Besides their interdisciplinary focus, there are three key elements of these programs. First, the programs have a significant focus on mission-based rather than disciplinary inquiry per se. Second, they adopt an ecological, social systems perspective on training that views behavioral development within the microsystems of family and school as well as the broader socioeconomic, community, policy, and cultural contexts that influence behavior in the microsystems. Finally, these programs focus on understanding the impact of program and policy interventions to promote human welfare. These are approached at different levels of analysis.

In the rest of this section, the programs are described through their mission, organization, and curriculum focus. Two student interviews are provided to illustrate experiences of students in implementing the programs.

Mission. Viewed broadly, the objectives of the programs include research, training, and public service within the contexts of the legal, family, school, community, and social service systems. The level of analysis in approaching these contexts also distinguishes these programs. For example, Nebraska's Law/Psychology Program and Wisconsin's Social Welfare Program emphasize policy analysis at the level of social systems including legal, governmental, and social welfare programs and policies. Students in the Law/Psychology Program may be interested in the effects of federal or supreme court decisions on individual or family behavior. Students in the social welfare program may be interested in analyzing the development and impact of welfare reform policies on family functioning.

Maryland's community-social program in human services psychology, Wisconsin's child and family studies program, and Penn State's intervention research program in human development emphasize investigation of the microsystems of family, school, and community on behavioral development as well as the causal processes of behavior and the effects of social programs. The community-social program focuses more on prevention programs and how "community structures" and "social resources" can be used to promote healthy behavior. The intervention research program emphasizes the design, implementation, and evaluation of comprehensive social programs. The emphasis of the child and family studies program is on understanding individual development within the contexts of the family and the broader social world and how this knowledge can be used to inform practice and the development of programs aimed at promoting human functioning and family well-being across the life span.

Organization. Table 2 displays the organizational structure of the programs. All provide training leading to the PhD, although Nebraska's Law/Psychology Program offers a joint PhD/JD program. All programs offer master's degrees but Wisconsin's social welfare program does not require it.

The programs differ somewhat in the number of core faculty. Nebraska and both Wisconsin programs have 14 faculty members, many of whom

TABLE 1. Program Mission Statements

Program	Mission Statement
U of Nebraska	The Law/Psychology Program offers interdisciplinary training in psychology and law. The program specializes in training scholars who will be able to apply psychology and other social and behavioral sciences to analyses of empirical questions in law and policy. The Law/Psychology Program trains researchers and professionals to identify and evaluate the psychological assumptions underlying laws and court decisions and to apply their psycho-legal expertise to improve understanding of the operation of law in society. Graduates of the Program are primarily trained to work in universities, research or public interest organizations, or in local state or federal government . . . The program does not offer training in the forensic/behavioral sciences designed to lead to careers in the FBI, the Secret Service, or other, similar law enforcement agencies.
Pennsylvania State U	Intervention research is the science of designing, implementing, and evaluating a broad array of approaches for improving the quality of life for individuals, families, and communities. Typically, interventions in HDFS are developmental in focus, meaning they are designed to prevent problems or to enhance healthy development, rather than to remediate long-standing personal, relational, or family problems. HDFS interventions often target the contexts in which people develop including families, schools, health and human service agencies, workplaces, and communities. Training in intervention research dovetails with the applied knowledge needed to conduct high quality interventions with methodological rigor (that is, rigor in areas such as measurement and assessment research design, and program evaluation).
University of Maryland at Baltimore County	Human Services Psychology is at Baltimore County defined as that sector of professional psychology concerned with the promotion of human well-being through the acquisition and application of psychological knowledge concerned with the diagnosis, treatment, and prevention of psychological and physical disorders. Thus, the program is designed to prepare students to contribute to the growth of knowledge in this area as well as to apply this knowledge to a broad range of human problems . . .

TABLE 1 (continued)

Program	Mission Statement
	The Human Services Psychology Program is an integrative structure encompassing three component specialty programs–behavioral medicine or health psychology, clinical psychology, and community social psychology . . . Community-Social Psychology focuses on the community structures, social resources, and human service policies which influence the effective functioning of both individuals and communities.
University of Wisconsin	The Child and Family Studies Graduate Program provides opportunities for advanced study and research on individual development, relationships, and families across the life span. Two assumptions are basic to the philosophy and organization of the program. First, individual development is best understood within the context of families. Second, understanding families is only possible within larger social contexts such as historical change, social class, ethnicity, public policy. The Child and Family Studies program offers courses on development in infancy, childhood, adolescence, adulthood, and old age. Other courses focus on family relationships, process, and diversity. The faculty bring the perspective of many different disciplines to their work. Faculty conduct basic and applied research to understand and enhance the development and well-being of individuals and family relationships. Some faculty are involved in advising public policy and family support projects. Faculty and students never lose sight of the connections among human development, family life, and broader sociohistorical contexts.
University of Wisconsin	The Ph.D. program in Social Welfare strives to develop scholars and educators who will advance knowledge about human welfare programs, policies, and practices. The program is interdisciplinary and research-oriented. The program is unique in that it is broadly interdisciplinary and highly individualized. Course work is taken in the School of Social Work and in other departments throughout the university. Students are expected to focus coursework in a field of study, a social problem area, or research on practice. The program offers proseminars at three levels of analysis: (a) policy-organizational behavior, (b) problem such as children, youth & families, mental health, and aging, and (c) program evaluation and practice. The purpose of these proseminars is to increase students' substantive knowledge and skills in applying social science theory and ability to apply research methods to social problems and issues.

TABLE 2. Program Descriptions

University	Department/School	Program	Degrees Offered	Core Faculty	Contact/Address
1. U of Nebraska at Lincoln	Psychology	Psychology and Law	Ph.D/J.D M.L.S.	14	Alan Tomkins, Lincoln, NE 68588; Ph. 402-472-2223
2. U of Maryland at Baltimore County	Psychology	Community-Social Psychology[a]	Ph.D., M.A.	4	Ken Maton, Baltimore, MD 21228; Ph. 410-455-2567
3. Pennsylvania State U at University Park	Human Development and Family Studies	Intervention Research	Ph.D., M.S.	6	Anthony D'Augelli, University Park, PA 16801; Ph. 814-863-0241
4. U of Wisconsin at Madison	Child and Family Studies	Same	Ph.D., M.A.	14	Stephen Small, Madison, WI 53706; Ph. 608-263-2381
5. U of Wisconsin at Madison	Social Work	Social Welfare	Ph.D., M.S.W.	14	Gary Seltzer, Madison, WI 53706; Ph. 608-263-3660

a = part of human services psychology program.
Note. The Penn State program is within the College of Health and Human Development. Wisconsin's Child and Family Studies Program is within the School of Human Ecology and the Social Welfare Program is within the College of Letters and Science.

are involved in community and applied research or have applied research interests. These numbers, however, do not take into account affiliated faculty with interests in the program. If this was taken into account, the Maryland and Penn State programs would be much larger. Notably, the University of Wisconsin programs included nearly the whole department since their research programs are defined as departments. This is not true of the other programs.

Curriculum Focus. Table 3 displays the curriculum of the five programs as well as the provision of practicum and internships. The number of students listed represent all currently active students in the department. Overall, the programs all require at least three courses in methodology and statistics as well as several proseminars in their major concentrations. As expected, students often participate in courses in affiliated departments. In both Wisconsin programs, for example, required statistics courses (and some methods courses) are regularly taken in other departments. Moreover, several faculty in child and family studies at Wisconsin have cooperative extension appointments and they serve as the core of the community research program. Brief program descriptions follow.

University of Nebraska. This joint program requires completion of five proseminars among an extensive list of psychology courses (e.g., community-clinical, social, developmental). In the PhD/JD program, more extensive coursework is required, although the MLS (master's in Legal Studies) also is an option. Elective courses are taken in sociology and educational psychology.

The University of Maryland offers course work in several areas that are consistent with those in traditional community psychology programs. These include community psychology, primary prevention, and evaluation research. Other course offerings include, among others, (taken as electives) law psychology, aggression, violence and crime, and planning theory and policy formulation.

Penn State University. In human development intervention, the four key courses are theories of human development intervention, consultation in human development, assessment, and evaluation research. These courses are taken in addition to courses in methodology as well as in individual and family development. Electives in other departments are encouraged, especially in methodology.

University of Wisconsin (Child and Family Studies). The content areas are typical of most programs in human development and family studies, although many courses focus on family issues. Theories and issues in human development, family theory, and several research methods courses are required. Students are also required to take a series of core content

TABLE 3. Ph.D. Program Curricula

University	Program Core Courses	Other Courses	Practicum/ Internship	No. of Students
1. U of Nebraska at Lincoln	Five Proseminars (e.g, Human Learning, clinical-community psych, social, history of philosophy) Law and Behavioral Science Psycholegal Research Topics in Law and Psychology Methodology Core Courses	Interdisciplinary courses Electives in Sociology, Psychology, Ed Psychology	required	30
2. U of Maryland at Baltimore County	Community Psychology Primary prevention Applied Social Psychology Public Policy Issues in Mental Health Evaluation Research Principles of Consultation Methodology Core Courses	Psychology and Law Psychology Aggression, Violence, & Crime Theories underlying admin. pract. Planning theory & policy formul.	required	134
3. Pennsylvania State U at University Park	Human Development Intervention Consultation in Human Devel Assessment in Human Devel Evaluation Research Methodology Core Courses	Intro to Human Development Family Development Advanced Child Development Electives in Sociology, Psychology, Statistics	encouraged	70
4. U of Wisconsin Child & Family Studies	Intro Proseminar Theories & Issues in Human Devel Family Theory I Statistics/Research Methods Specialization courses	Electives in Sociology, Ed Psych, Social Work, Nursing CFS courses such as Family Policy, Violence, Alcohol & the Family, and evaluation research	encouraged	46
5. U of Wisconsin Social Welfare	Four Proseminars in policy/ organizational behavior, social problem areas (poverty, disabilities, (mental health, children, youth & families, and aging), and practice/program evaluation Research Methods/Statistics Core Courses	Electives in Sociology, Ed Psych, Child & Family Studies, Psychology	required	45

Note. The student totals are for the entire department, not the program.

courses in their area of interest. A sample of such courses include infancy and the family, childhood and the family, and adolescence and life-span social development. Students may also take course work in program development, evaluation, social policy, and methods for translating research into practice. Required statistics courses are mostly taken in the sociology and educational psychology departments.

University of Wisconsin (Social Welfare). Unlike the above programs, the social welfare program is highly interdisciplinary and individualized. Four proseminars are required and they include the areas of organizational behavior, social policy, poverty, developmental disabilities, mental health/illness, and children, youth and families as well as program/policy evaluation. Research methods and statistics are largely taken in sociology and educational psychology departments. Elective courses are taken in several departments. Most students in the PhD program have a master's degree in social work, which requires an internship or field placement.

STUDENT INTERVIEWS

To highlight the content and focus of interdisciplinary programs, summaries of two interviews with current students are provided below. The first is a beginning student and the second is a finishing student.

Interview 1: Current Student in Child and Family Studies, University of Wisconsin at Madison

1. Why did you decide on this program for your doctoral education?

I decided on a Child and Family Studies Department because of the interdisciplinary nature of the program. Coming into the program with a EdM in Counseling Psychology, I wanted a department that would match my interests yet expand my knowledge about the family system in both an applied and research context.

I chose the program at the University of Wisconsin-Madison for various reasons. One of the most important reasons was because of the research interests of the faculty. In addition, I was matched with an Advisor who has extensive research experience in the area I want to pursue. I also chose this particular program because of its affiliation with the Waisman Center, an educational center which provides services to developmentally delayed populations and supports a wide variety of research working with individuals with special needs. Finally, I chose this university because of its highly respected reputation and the vast range of opportunities this large university is able to provide.

2. What significant work/educational experiences did you come into the program with?

I received my EdM in Counseling Psychology at the Graduate School of Education, Rutgers University. This program allowed me to pursue my interests in applied settings. I also received an Infant Specialist Certificate to work with children birth through five years of age. As part of my program, I took course work that focused on all developmental aspects of children under five and their families. I also took counseling classes related to infant-parent therapy and family counseling. Furthermore, my graduate training consisted of a practicum where I worked in Early Intervention Services for a year. In addition, after graduating, I received a paid summer position working in a preschool for autistic children.

3. What do you like/have you liked most about your program so far?

I really appreciate the mentoring that the faculty in Child and Family Studies extends to the students in the program. I enjoy that the program is small enough so that each student receives individualized attention, yet large enough so that professional and personal networks are able to develop. In addition, I like the diversity within the department and broad range of ideas that each faculty member contributes to the program. I also like the vast amount of research opportunities available to students.

I do not like that more applied areas of research are not encouraged in the program. It is difficult to receive credits toward your degree through practicum experience. Furthermore, classes are often too research based without focusing on implications research has on policy issues or in applied settings.

4. Which content or course work focus has been/will be most important in your doctoral education?

The statistics and methodological classes offered will provide me with a strong knowledge base in research methods. In addition, taking classes in human development theory and family theory will provide me background in which to apply my research ideas. Moreover, due to the interdisciplinary make-up of the faculty, classes, presentations, and informal gatherings allow me greater understanding of different areas of research.

5. What are your specific interests in research and in policy/program intervention?

I am interested in at risk children's early educational experiences and how those experiences translate to later competence. In addition, a focus of interest is determining what family components affect children's educational experiences.

Subsequently, I am interested in how parent's incorporate educational experiences, especially intervention services, into the home environment. Moreover, the relationship between the home environment and the educational setting, particularly early intervention programs, has been primarily studied at the school level. I am interested in researching the relationship between parent-child interactions at home and how that translates into interventions sought and the success of those educational experiences.

6 (a). What are your professional plans upon graduation?

Ideally, I would like to begin work in an applied setting. I would like to work with parents and their children at risk (whether it be a special needs population or a disadvantaged population) and provide supportive intervention services. I would also like to be involved in evaluation of programs that offer such services to determine the most effective intervention methods, on both a psycho-social domain and an educational level.

I would like to divide my time doing applied work, teaching at a university, and research. However, I do not envision myself initially working at a university to obtain tenure. I want to work directly with the population I research for a number of years before I dedicate most of my time to the duties of a tenure track professor.

(b). How about in ten years?

I see myself working in intervention services, and at the beginning of more involvement in university duties.

Interview 2: Current Student in Social Welfare, University of Wisconsin-Madison

1. Why did you decide on this program for your doctoral education?

Studying social work reflects my career and life goals in relation to my (Christian) values and aptitude. I decided to pursue a PhD in order to advance my own research ability and knowledge in my field concentration as well as general areas of social welfare. I chose this university primarily because of the professors with whom I could collaborate on the study. At the time I entered this program, we had a few faculty members who I shared similar interests with, but all of them have left this university, including my former advisor.

2. What significant work/educational experiences did you come into the program with?

Because I had worked with people who had been in abusive environments at the Domestic Abuse Project in MSW program, I realized what I wanted to do in my life, and the doctoral program has taught me what being a scholar and a researcher is like.

3. What do you like/have you liked most about your program so far?

It may be an unexpected answer, but one thing that I like most about my program is the professors in the university. Even though I do not have any guidance with respect to the fields of domestic violence, the professors that I know have shown me the mentorship I need to be a teacher, researcher, and the kind of human being I want to be in future. Their academic expectations for students are quite reasonable (it is challenging but not inhuman). The university offers an excellent environment for learning the research method.

4. Which content or coursework focus has been/will be most important in your doctoral education?

The courses related to research methods are important in this PhD program partly due to the SW curriculum that stresses research knowledge and skills. The courses I took were all connected to research methods in various ways. Although I am pleased to have such educational training (and I still need to improve this area), I am sorry that I could not have more opportunities to develop my other career goals, such as learning counseling techniques and theories or having related working experiences. Emphasizing research in the doctoral program has, for me, raised questions about the possible loss of a more "human" sense of social work's essence. Another issue lies in what degree of knowledge we should deepen in each study area. Considering the characteristic of social work (e.g., a preference for broad knowledge), it is understandable, but I, personally, am not satisfied with the level of expertise in each specific area. A lack of courses on theories is my other concern.

5. What are your specific interests in research and in policy/program intervention?

Within my major field in the MSW and doctoral program, my primary concern has been centered around domestic violence in general and woman abuse in particular. Thus, I am interested in doing research that will be connected to social work practice in the area of family violence. In the beginning of my field of concentration, my knowledge and working experiences had been directed to female victims of partner abuse; however, I have recently shifted my major focus to the studies of men who batter. My research interests are in developing more effective intervention strategies for abusive men in order for them to change their violent behavior. A related clinical research interest is to explore the potential effectiveness of group treatment methods designed for group members who have certain problems in common, particularly offenders or victims of a variety of abuse (e.g., child abuse, sexual abuse, etc.). Besides clinical interventions, I am also interested in other factors which could contribute to reducing violence, such as criminal justice programs, legislation, policy and public attitudes or opinion.

6 (a). What are your professional plans upon graduation?

Although I cannot make a near-future plan at present, I have lifetime professional goals. The long-term goal is to inaugurate programs for domestic abuse issues in Korea; to influence professional, official and public opinion about woman abuse; to work for change in the law and policy about women and children who are living in violence; and to build the organization necessary for the families experiencing violence. My role as an educator, researcher, and clinician would help create an "environment" for innovating and developing a social welfare program addressing domestic violence. I will need to bring out the problem by research and education, and work to make domestic violence a social problem in public, the government and the society. To be able to start programs for abusers, some kinds of domestic abuse acts would be established. My ultimate professional goals are to train and develop clinical programs for men, women, and children who are in violent relationships (It is too ambitious!).

(b). Where do you see yourself in ten years?

Well, though it seems too far ahead to imagine clearly, I might teach at a university in Korea, do research, (hopefully) work with my study population, and struggle with culture and government. Whatever I do I imagine I would be quite busy with people and tasks.

Program Development

Interdisciplinary programs in social and behavioral research are consistent with many trends in the social sciences and seek to use scientific inquiry to promote human welfare. This interdisciplinary or multidisciplinary focus is reflected in each of the programs, especially in human development and family studies programs and in social welfare. Two areas appear particularly promising for further program development: prevention research and program evaluation.

Prevention Research is the scientific study, through multiple methodologies, of systematic efforts to reduce the incidence of maladaptive behavior and to promote adaptive behavior in populations across the life span. Major characteristics are that it is (a) mission-based rather than disciplinary-based, (b) promotes healthy development and ameliorates problematic development, (c) focuses on primary and secondary strategies rather than tertiary ones, and (d) emphasizes the dissemination of research findings to policy and practice.

Evaluation Research is the "systematic application of social research procedures for assessing the conceptualization, design, implementation, and utility of social intervention programs" (Rossi and Freeman, 1993, p. 5). Major characteristics are comprehensive approaches; quantitative, qualitative, and mixed methodologies; improving causal inference through research design and statistical analysis; and tailoring evaluation designs to stage of program development.

An Illustration

Interestingly, one of the programs (Penn State) has made substantial efforts to facilitate the development of training in these areas. Through discussion among faculty and students, review of existing programs, a program proposal was developed in prevention and program evaluation. The development of such programs would add significantly to the interdisciplinary flavor of community research and action. One recommendation would be to implement programs in these and related areas. A proposed mission statement for an interdisciplinary program at Penn State University reads as follows.

Sample Mission Statement

The goal of the Prevention Research and Program Evaluation emphasis is to train students in the field of prevention science and in comprehensive approaches to evaluation of programmatic efforts from a social problem perspective. The major focus of the program is to critically examine the conceptualization and development of preventive interventions from a multidisciplinary perspective and to engage in sophisticated analyses of the design, implementation, and effects of developmental interventions.

Prevention and evaluation research in this program has three special features. First, an emphasis is given to programmatic approaches that seek to prevent the development of problematic outcomes and to promote optimal functioning in individuals or groups across the life span. Second, we stress that preventive interventions are implemented and evaluated in family, school, and community contexts; their impact should be investigated in interaction with these contexts. Finally, we emphasize methodological and statistical training and their applications in evaluation research of interventions.

Expertise Acquired

- Conceptualizing and developing innovative approaches to ameliorating social problems such as school failure, delinquency, and other problem behaviors
- Consulting with human-service, governmental, and educational organizations in the design and evaluation of social programs or policies
- Evaluating social programs that are based in the context of families, schools, and communities
- Identifying the causes and consequences of significant developmental outcomes
- Developing new approaches to the analysis of prevention programs and their effectiveness
- Translating research findings into policy and program practice

Faculty Research Emphases

- Improving access to prenatal and postnatal care
- Investigating longitudinal effects of early childhood programs
- Improving social functioning of at-risk youth
- Preventing drug abuse, delinquency, and AIDS
- Enhancing problem-solving skills in older adults
- Studying the impact of daycare services for dementia patients and their caregivers
- Estimating the effects of prevention programs on life-span development
- Identifying risk and protective factors in development

CONCLUSION

Interdisciplinary training in community research and action has grown substantially across the social and behavioral sciences. The development of such training programs in organizations such as the Council of Program Directors in Community Research and Action is important in broadening the focus and visibility of community psychology and related areas. Although each of the five programs described are distinct in focus, they are surprisingly consistent with the mission statement reproduced at the beginning of this article. Two domains that are particularly promising are in prevention research and program evaluation. The development of new programs in community research and the associated fields of human development, social work and welfare, and evaluation would add significantly to research, scholarship, and training in interdisciplinary community research on the social problems and contexts that affect individuals and groups.

Starting an Interdisciplinary Program

Those interested in starting an interdisciplinary program in community or intervention related areas should first consult with existing programs to develop an understanding of key factors and processes that provided the impetus for program development. Once the history and objectives of the programs are understood, a guiding framework or focus of the prospective program should be developed which addresses an important scientific or social need. Often, developing a niche in a specialty area of community-related research is a primary interest. This was especially the case for the law-psychology program at the University of Nebraska and the intervention research program at Penn State University (also see Fisher et al., 1993). As noted above, prevention research and program evaluation are examples of key areas for which programs could be designed. After agreement on program focus (comprehensive or specific) and relevant disciplines to be included, a critical mass of faculty would need to be identified. Developing a mission statement, designing core courses, and recruiting students would then become primary. Regarding graduate program content, Table 3 lists many possible course titles and foci. Establishing collaborative relationships with like-minded research institutes and centers or with local agencies (e.g., health and human services, school systems) could be useful in providing internships and additional research opportunities.

REFERENCES

American Psychological Society. (1995, March). The Human Capital Initiative: Opportunities for human capital research. *APS Observer,* 40.

Bornstein, M. H. (1995). A "new look" at Child Development. *Child Development, 66,* Editorial.

Coie, J. et al. (1993). The science of prevention: A conceptual framework and some directions for a national research program. *American Psychologist, 48,* 1013-1023.

Fisher, C. B. et al. (1993). The national conference on graduate education in the applications of developmental science across the life span. *Journal of Applied Developmental Psychology, 14,* 1-10.

Rossi, P. H., & Freeman, H. E. (1993). *Evaluation: A systematic approach* (5th ed.). Thousand Oaks, CA: Sage.

Developing a Graduate Program in Community Psychology: Experiences at the University of Waikato, New Zealand

David R. Thomas
Beth Neill
Neville Robertson
University of Waikato

The Department of Psychology at the University of Waikato in New Zealand is located in the School of Social Sciences. The Department offers specialized study in social, industrial-organizational, cross-cultural, community and clinical psychology. Other Social Sciences programs include: health studies, women's studies and environmental planning. Community Psychology is offered as a specialization in the Master of Social Sciences degree, as a professional training program for a three-year Post Graduate Diploma in Psychology, and as an area of doctoral study.

The Community Psychology Diploma program commenced in 1980 with three students. At the end of 1995 there were 38 graduates from the program and 24 students enrolled for the community psychology Diploma. The Diploma Program was accredited in February 1990 by the New Zealand Psychological Society. Graduates from the Diploma program may become registered psychologists.

Address correspondence to the authors at the University of Waikato, Private Bag 3105, Hamilton, New Zealand.

[Haworth co-indexing entry note]: "Developing a Graduate Program in Community Psychology: Experiences at the University of Waikato, New Zealand." Thomas, David R., Beth Neill, and Neville Robertson. Co-published simultaneously in *Journal of Prevention & Intervention in the Community* (The Haworth Press, Inc.) Vol. 15, No. 1, 1997, pp. 83-95; and: *Education in Community Psychology: Models for Graduate and Undergraduate Programs* (ed: Clifford R. O'Donnell, and Joseph R. Ferrari.) The Haworth Press, Inc., 1997, pp. 83-95. Single or multiple copies of this article are available for a fee from The Haworth Document Delivery Service [1-800-342-9678, 9:00 a.m. - 5:00 p.m. (EST). E-mail address: getinfo@haworth.com].

The Community Psychology graduate program has record of collaborating with community organizations on evaluations, policy-related research, organizational development, and community needs surveys. The program has links with community and national organizations, such as alcohol and family counseling services, community houses, women's refuges, women's health centres, local government, regional health authorities, and the central government departments. The University is located in a region with a considerable proportion of Maori people (the indigenous people of New Zealand). Faculty and students are regularly involved in research with Maori groups.

CHALLENGES IN SETTING UP THE PROGRAM

In its early years other social sciences faculty were often indifferent towards the program and a few were hostile towards it. Since then the program has become accepted as a regular part of the graduate training in psychology. We now get other social science faculty, who are establishing new graduate programs, seeking advice.

An early concern was developing a professional identity for graduates and a sense of security about jobs being available for graduates after they completed their training. Currently community graduates have better job prospects after graduation than clinical psychology students.

In the program we worked on establishing a sense of group identity, especially among new students joining the program. A supportive network was developed among students through specific activities such as: social evenings, field trips to community agencies outside Hamilton, and a requirement that students do some of their graduate work in group projects. We consider it important to establish contact between new students and those who have been in the program for a year or more.

During the last ten years the identity of the program has become better established for several reasons:

- we have developed extensive links with local human service organizations through involvement of our graduates, by inviting staff as guest speakers, and through joint social functions.
- the program has developed a track record for applied research and we get regular requests from community agencies asking for graduates to do research.
- graduates working in human service agencies are employing intern students.

- agencies regularly contact the program looking for community psychology graduates to fill vacant positions.

CORE KNOWLEDGE AND SKILLS

During a program review in 1995, we developed a detailed description of the knowledge base and skills relevant to community psychology. The topics listed below identify the core of the knowledge base for the community psychology program with which graduates are expected to be familiar. The list provides a context for learning objectives and assessment in the professional practice papers in the graduate program.

VALUES AND PRINCIPLES

Values are inextricably enmeshed in all forms of human behavior, including psychological research and practice. Core values and principles which have been identified in community psychology are: empowerment, social justice, diversity and cultural pluralism, cultural awareness, social innovation, evaluation, community development, community participation and collaboration.

Empowerment and Competence Enhancement

Empowerment has become one of the key themes in community psychology. It has been defined as enhancing the possibility that people can more actively control their own lives. The growth of a psychological sense of personal control and concern with social influence, political power, and legal rights are inherent in empowerment. Social change interventions need to emphasize the development of strengths, competencies and skills rather than just describing deficits, weaknesses and needs.

Social Justice

Social justice involves planning social change interventions which benefit people who are experiencing disadvantage. Such interventions may involve: highlighting inequities in the ways human services operate, providing access to resources and support services, and changing services that discriminate against non-dominant groups.

Diversity and Cultural Pluralism

Community psychologists value human diversity. Differences, in culture, gender, class, sexual orientation or (dis)ability should be recognized and respected, and people should be free to express their cultural values and participate in all spheres of life. This enhances the quality of life for people within diverse societies. Cultural pluralism follows from the belief in the positive nature of human diversity and the right to be different without suffering material or psychological sanctions. Indigenous peoples have the right to self-determination for their communities. The belief in cultural pluralism is constrained by the proviso that the expression of cultural or religious values must not infringe on the rights of other groups or deny the validity of individual rights.

Cultural Awareness and Biculturalism

Community psychologists need to have an understanding of the process of colonization and its impact on colonized people, especially in relation to the colonization of New Zealand. We need to develop social, political and economic processes which are consistent with the spirit and intentions of the Treaty of Waitangi. This involves an appreciation of Maori concerns, the development of bicultural skills, and supporting self-determination for Maori iwi (tribes) and communities.

Social Innovation

Community psychologists promote the use of innovative techniques and approaches to deal with recurrent social problems, recognizing that some existing approaches are ineffective, or make social problems worse. Reducing social problems can often be achieved by changing environmental conditions as well as strategies that focus on changing the behavior of individuals.

Evaluation

Evaluation of social action is seen as an essential part of social change and innovation. Evaluation can identify positive and negative effects of social change strategies and provide information for decision-making. Evaluation is important because resources are usually limited and need to be used as efficiently as possible.

Community Development and Participation

Community development refers to a process of strengthening a community's human, economic and environmental resources with the goal of creating a 'healthy' or 'competent' community. A healthy community can reduce social and psychological problems and enable members to grow to their maximum potential. Community development is more likely to occur if residents identify with community activities and are committed to local concerns. Residents should be able to participate in assessment of needs and setting of priorities in matters affecting their communities.

Collaboration and Partnership

In terms of social interventions, long-term positive changes require work practices which involve collaboration and partnership. Community psychologists value the knowledge, skills and experience of others. Partnerships with community groups are preferred, where each partner contributes; for example, in the setting of research objectives and the ways in which the research findings are used.

An Ecological Approach

An ecological approach recognizes the importance of environmental and situational processes in maintaining social problems. Growing understanding of the influence of environmental factors on behavior has seen community psychology link more closely with environmental psychology and human geography.

Systems Perspectives

A further aspect of the field of community psychology, related to understanding environmental and organizational influences on behavior, is knowledge about how social systems operate. Systems perspectives involve the concepts of multiple causation of social problems, multiple levels of analysis, and interventions at the levels of organizational, institutional and community systems.

Prevention

In most human services, distinctions are made between prevention and treatment. For many social problems, such as substance abuse, most resources are allocated to treatment services. Community based disciplines focus more broadly on preventive interventions.

PROFESSIONAL ROLES AND PRACTICE

The roles of *consultant, researcher, networker, trainer, evaluator, policy analyst, planner, negotiator,* and *facilitator* are relevant to the practice of community psychology. Individually these roles are not unique to community psychology, nor do all community psychologists use all of these roles. However they provide an indication of the range of activities which characterize community psychology.

Two specific topics which are relevant to professional practice for community psychologists in New Zealand are: registration under the New Zealand Psychologist's Act (1981) and the Code of Ethics of the New Zealand Psychological Society.

COMPETENCIES AND SKILLS

Some examples of the competencies and skills which we have been found to be important for community psychologists are outlined below. These skills are categorized into three broad groups: *technical skills, collaboration skills* and *personal effectiveness skills.* While not all practitioners will develop these skills to the same extent, the list does gives an indication of the range of competencies that community psychologists might expect to develop during their training and early work experience.

Technical Skills

Project Management

- Conceptualization of a project including: assessing needs, defining problems to be addressed and establishing project parameters.
- Developing a project plan including task analysis, setting priorities, developing a budget, drawing up agreements.
- Managing resources, monitoring progress, resolving differences, delivering on agreements and evaluating outcomes.
- Time management; efficient management of one's own time and other staff for whom one has supervisory responsibility.
- Planning effectively, determining priorities, meeting deadlines.

Research Skills

- Being able to write effective research proposals and funding applications.
- Conducting literature reviews.
- Conducting applied research using both qualitative and quantitative research methods.
- Familiarity with interviewing techniques and questionnaire construction.

- Familiarity with computers and data analysis for qualitative and quantitative data.

Evaluation Skills

- Working with organizations to clarify what they need to evaluate.
- Develop methods to monitor service effectiveness.
- Assessment of organizational and service effectiveness.
- Providing information to improve services.

Policy Analysis

- Understanding of policy formulation, implementation and evaluation.
- Being able to critique policy.
- Synthesizing a broad range of information and developing options.
- Understanding the operation of local, regional and central government.
- Understanding legislation relevant to community psychology (e.g., children and families, local government).

Collaboration Skills

Training and Consultation Skills

- Working with participants in communities and organizations to assess their training needs, developing, implementing and evaluating training programs.
- Being able to conduct effective workshops, seminars and training forums.

Negotiation and Mediation Skills

- Being able to retain impartiality when acting as a mediator.
- Sensitive to the needs of other groups in negotiations.
- Clarifying issues on which there is agreement.
- Mediating conflict, establishing effective communication to improve organizational effectiveness.

Bicultural and Multicultural Skills

- Being familiar with the use of Maori protocol.
- Using bicultural practices when appropriate.

- Avoiding behaviors likely to cause offense or misunderstanding for specific cultural groups.

Networking and Partnership Skills

- Maintaining relationships with a range of community organizations.
- Building links between people and groups in the community.
- Identifying and facilitating access to resources in the community.
- Working with local people and communities to help meet their objectives.
- Building non-traditional alliances for projects that stimulate positive changes.

Personal Effectiveness Skills

Communication Skills

- Being able to write clearly for a variety of audiences (e.g., formal correspondence, grant applications, research reports, executive summaries, press releases, policy analyses, submissions, literature reviews, academic journal articles, non-academic magazine items).
- Report writing; including overview of issues, integrating information, presenting it clearly for organizational, public and political decision-making.
- Public speaking: being comfortable addressing both large and small groups and making oral presentations that are appropriate for specific audiences.

Interpersonal Skills

- Being able to relate easily to people from a variety of backgrounds–including groups which vary in culture, class, gender, sexual orientation.
- Basic counseling skills (reflective listening, clarifying, questioning).
- Being able to communicate clearly in diverse settings.
- Conflict management and resolution skills (negotiation, mediation).

Organizational Skills

- Skills in keeping records, time keeping, personal presentation and supervision.
- Negotiating tasks and workloads with supervisors and other staff.

- Team-work skills: an ability to negotiate joint tasks, clarify roles, work collaboratively and resolve conflicts in a respectful manner.
- Being aware of and responding appropriately to political or interpersonal conflict among others within an organization or department.
- Use of computers, including electronic mail networks and accessing information.

Support and Coping

- Seeking out and utilizing appropriate support and supervision from colleagues, supervisors and others.
- Developing appropriate strategies for handling stress.
- Being able to manage workloads and resist pressures to take on too much work.
- Taking time out when necessary to avoid burnout.

MAINTAINING THE PROGRAM

Several challenges are likely to occur within any graduate program, particularly in the early years. These challenges need to be addressed in ways which facilitate program survival and long-term development. Challenges include justification for faculty appointments, threats of program termination, staff burnout, and conflict among program staff. These have been issues at the University of Waikato.

In the mid-1980s enrollments in some subjects were declining. New programs, such as community psychology, came under close scrutiny when core program faculty resigned. At one stage there were calls to close the program because it was too "expensive" in terms of teaching resources. We survived both of these challenges as a result of intensive lobbying.

It is expected that faculty teaching within the community psychology program will hold different perspectives on a number of issues. When students become involved in conflicts between faculty, it leads to lower morale among both faculty and students. One strategy for dealing with differences relevant to academic matters is to have an open forum where the various different perspectives are presented directly to students.

Other issues relevant to program maintenance and development include: there is always more program development work needed than there is faculty time available, the importance of close supervision of graduate students working in applied settings, and helping students manage conflict in their work settings.

PROGRAM REVIEWS

Since the program began in 1980, there have been four major reviews: in late 1982, during 1984-85, during 1986-87 in preparation for the submission for accreditation, and in 1995. The program reviews have provided important information in addition to the regular course evaluations which are carried out at the end of the teaching year. Changes resulting from program reviews have included:

- ensuring the work required was more evenly distributed among courses.
- changing a practical course from completion of a community intervention project to short placement visits to three human service agencies.
- revision of the internship requirements to better reflect the diversity of internship settings and ensure assessment procedures were relevant to internship settings.
- revision of the knowledge and skills for the Community Psychology Handbook.

THE EXPERIENCES OF GRADUATES

Employment Opportunities

Graduates from the University of Waikato program have taken up positions as community psychologists in health services, community service organizations, government departments and in private practice. Over the last few years there has been a continuing demand for graduates with community psychology skills. Most graduates have little difficulty in finding employment. An increasingly common option in the 1990s, since the restructuring of health and welfare services in New Zealand, is for graduates to become involved in contract work with human service organizations. Employment taken up by graduates has included:

- Health Promotion Officer, regional health authority
- Accident researcher and safety advisor
- Community Services, Department of Social Welfare
- Private Practice
- Evaluation researchers, research organizations
- Planners in regional and city councils
- Community alcohol and drug services

Student Expectations and Views of the Program

As part of the most recent program review, students were interviewed about their expectations when they entered the program, their learning experiences so far, and what they wanted from program staff. Their views are summarized in this section.

The aspirations of students entering the program are diverse. When graduates were asked what attracted them to the program, the opportunity to become registered psychologists sat alongside the chance to learn how to work effectively for social change. Their expectations of the program are high, both in terms of professional development, and its contribution to social justice.

Students expect to learn evaluation research skills, and the program has built a reputation for providing excellent training opportunities in this area. Policy analysis is of increasing interest to students, and there is also an ongoing interest in the challenges that postmodernism and feminist perspectives provide for community psychology.

Students also want to develop effective professional skills which will enable them to practice in settings as diverse as government policy-making agencies, community and tribally-based groups, or in private practice.

Program faculty integrate the values of community psychology into teaching and management processes. We emphasize collaborative work; students are required to work on joint as well as individual projects. Students who know about difficulties with group projects think it is important that staff recognize the extra demands placed on students when they are required to work cooperatively in an individualistic environment.

Faculty are expected to work collaboratively with students, as well providing close supervision of students working in community settings. While both faculty and students value the nature of the relationship they have with each other, students note that it is important they feel free to raise issues they have about the program, or about their involvements with community agencies and groups.

One of the challenges for students is to maintain their vision of community psychology once they move from primarily meeting university course requirements within the University, to work in organizations that might not share community psychology perspectives. This transition usually means that students need a high level of support and guidance in the initial stages of working in a community agency.

PROGRAM DEVELOPMENT AND CHANGE

A challenge for the program has been to continuously develop the program and teaching materials so they are consistent with changes in students' expectations, job opportunities, new legislation affecting human services, and changes in the social, cultural and political environments in New Zealand. Some trends are outlined below.

Program Documentation

Increasingly students expect that detailed information will be provided in program documents. Building on accumulated experiences considerable time has gone into development of written materials used for general information and instructional purposes. Completed graduate research reports are made available to new students.

Changes in Employment Patterns

In the early 1980s most graduates expected to go into a full-time salaried position. With privatization of government services, many graduates now find work through contracts and other time-limited employment opportunities. These students need to construct budgets, handle financial matters, tender for contracts and manage project administration. Increasingly students are seeking these skills within the program.

Changes in Values, Lifestyles and Expectations

In recent years about 80-90% of graduate students entering the program are women. There has been a strong demand from some graduates for incorporation of feminist perspectives within the program. This has been met by employment of a faculty member who can provide these skills and perspectives.

Another dominant theme, reflecting wider changes in New Zealand society, has been an increasing emphasis on biculturalism and cultural diversity in relation to the dominant Pakeha (New Zealanders of European descent) and indigenous Maori peoples. There has been considerable effort to recruit Maori graduate students and Maori faculty contribute to the graduate program.

IMPLICATIONS FOR DEVELOPING COMMUNITY PSYCHOLOGY PROGRAMS

The following points may be relevant to other community psychology programs.

Expect the Program to Evolve

New programs evolve over time. Expect changes to occur and build the process for change into program planning and reviews. In our courses we would expect to change about 20% of the readings and topics each year so after five years the course will look very different. Having regular program reviews helps faculty take stock of what they are doing and plan revisions. We have found feedback from students who have completed the program to be crucial for program improvement.

Develop a Program Identity and Track Record

In the early stage of a program's development few people will know about the program, what it might do for them, or who to contact. As the program became more widely known, requests for graduate student involvement in evaluations and offers of employment have steadily increased. One indicator of a program's visibility is the number of applicants for entry to the program who are studying at other universities.

Develop Networks with Human Service Organizations

Developing an effective community psychology program depends on establishing an extensive network of contacts with local and regional human service organizations. Some procedures we have used include: inviting human services staff as guest speakers and for social functions, by requesting opportunities for our students to do short placements, and by carrying out research which is useful for the organizations.

Undergraduate Courses and Graduate Programs in Community Research and Action: Issues and Future Directions

Clifford R. O'Donnell

University of Hawaii

Joseph R. Ferrari

DePaul University

The authors of these articles have presented an excellent review, with many examples, of undergraduate courses and graduate programs in community research and action. Particularly important are the types of knowledge and skills that are taught, the professional roles available for community graduates, the importance of close working relationships with community organizations, the steps and issues to consider when planning a community course or program, and the possible future directions of education in community research and action.

The range of knowledge and skills taught is remarkable. In addition to the typical values of research and scholarship, is the value of responsibility to the community and to social justice; to the typical methodology, is the need for field and naturalistic methods; to quantitative analysis, is qualitative analysis; to individual treatment, is prevention, empowerment, consultation, negotiation, and social intervention; to assessment, is program

[Haworth co-indexing entry note]: "Undergraduate Courses and Graduate Programs in Community Research and Action: Issues and Future Directions." O'Donnell, Clifford R., and Joseph R. Ferrari. Co-published simultaneously in *Journal of Prevention & Intervention in the Community* (The Haworth Press, Inc.) Vol. 15, No. 1, 1997, pp. 97-99; and: *Education in Community Psychology: Models for Graduate and Undergraduate Programs* (ed: Clifford R. O'Donnell, and Joseph R. Ferrari.) The Haworth Press, Inc., 1997, pp. 97-99. Single or multiple copies of this article are available for a fee from The Haworth Document Delivery Service [1-800-342-9678, 9:00 a.m. - 5:00 p.m. (EST). E-mail address: getinfo@haworth.com].

evaluation and policy analysis; to sensitivity to the differences of others, is the need for the cultural compatibility of programs; and to developing rapport with others, is the necessity of collaboration with community members.

Given this range of knowledge and skills, it is understandable that community graduates have opportunities for many different professional roles. These roles, however, often are not labeled "psychologist," and this has contributed to the myth that there are not many jobs for non-clinical community graduates. Programs report that their graduates find employment in community social services, advocacy organizations, government planning agencies, and consultation firms, in addition to colleges, universities, and research centers.

For both undergraduate courses and graduate programs, the authors noted the importance of developing collaborative relationships with community organizations. These relationships are helpful to develop community projects, student field placements, student financial support, graduate employment, and community program support. Thomas, Neill, and Robertson (in this issue) suggested that social functions that include faculty, students, and community agency staff members can help to develop and maintain these relationships. Community staff members also frequently can serve on thesis and dissertation committees, and participate in student selection, placement, and curriculum decisions.

The many types of community courses and programs offer flexible opportunities to develop undergraduate courses and graduate programs even with minimal resources. The Community Psychology Education Connection Clearinghouse is available to provide references, syllabi, and related materials for course development. Community agencies and other disciplines can be valuable sources of graduate faculty and the cross-listing of courses in related disciplines can supplement core curriculum. Master's and doctoral programs could develop their links to each other, and articulate their curricula to attract students who wish to continue for a doctoral degree. Both students and programs could benefit from such arrangements. The suggestions the authors made offer practical guidance for those who wish to develop community courses and programs at their institutions.

Perhaps the most interesting aspect of these articles is the implication for the future direction of education in community research and action. The change in APA guidelines and procedures in accreditation, the drive for prescription privileges, the growing effect of managed-care, and the internship/employment crisis for clinical psychology will have a major impact on community research and action. This impact will occur both within psychology and in interdisciplinary programs. Within psychology, it appears that clinical-community programs will be under pressure to become a medicalized, individual/small group, clinical-treatment program dependent on third-party payers or to join with their community psychology colleagues to create a professional psychology program focused on prevention, empowerment, consultation, negotiation, social intervention, program evaluation, policy, and community development.

Outside of psychology, the growth of interdisciplinary community graduate programs offers an alternative for psychologists who seek to emphasize community psychology and desire freedom from the restrictions of a medicalized clinical psychology. Interdisciplinary programs offer the intellectual perspectives, students, faculty, and resources of several disciplines. They tend to be mission rather than discipline-oriented and can offer graduates employment possibilities in several fields.

Overall, these articles show that the ecological conditions are changing and many new opportunities are being created. It is an exciting time to be involved in community research and action.

Index

Page numbers followed by t indicate tables.

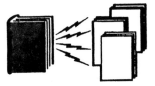

COSTS: Please figure your cost to order quality copies of an article.

1. Set-up charge per article: $8.00
   ($8.00 × number of separate articles) ________
2. Photocopying charge for each article:
   1-10 pages: $1.00 ________
   11-19 pages: $3.00 ________
   20-29 pages: $5.00 ________
   30+ pages: $2.00/10 pages ________
3. Flexicover (optional): $2.00/article ________
4. Postage & Handling: US: $1.00 for the first article/
   $.50 each additional article ________
   Federal Express: $25.00 ________
   Outside US: $2.00 for first article/
   $.50 each additional article ________
5. Same-day FAX service: $.35 per page ________

GRAND TOTAL: ________

METHOD OF PAYMENT: (please check one)

❑ Check enclosed ❑ Please ship and bill. PO # ________
(sorry we can ship and bill to bookstores only! All others must pre-pay)

❑ Charge to my credit card: ❑ Visa; ❑ MasterCard; ❑ Discover; ❑ American Express;

Account Number: ________ Expiration date: ________

Signature: ✗ ________

Name: ________ Institution: ________

Address: ________

____

City: ________ State: ________ Zip: ________

Phone Number: ________ FAX Number: ________

MAIL or *FAX* THIS ENTIRE ORDER FORM TO:

Haworth Document Delivery Service
The Haworth Press, Inc.
10 Alice Street
Binghamton, NY 13904-1580

or FAX: 1-800-895-0582
or CALL: 1-800-342-9678
9am-5pm EST)